What gets measured gets done

Unveiling the secrets of performance management

Nopadol Rompho

Preface

Simon Sinek makes a particularly interesting point in his book Start With Why: How Great Leaders Inspire Everyone to Take Action. The author lays down the three important questions: what, how, and why. Most people only communicate the "what" and "how," failing to address the "why." I could have written in this preface: "This book is about performance management (the what); and will present how it is designed and put to good use in organizations (the how)." Then, this would be an ordinary book about performance management techniques. However, I'd like to communicate the "why" first. I am inspired to transform the usual jargon-filled "academic textbook" into an engaging and comprehensible text. I studied many excellent research reports that few people manage to get through, and saw many useful textbooks gather dust on library shelves. My aim is to transform such content into simple terms that everyone can comprehend, and more importantly, enjoy.

Through my experience of teaching, writing textbooks, and researching about performance management made, I realized that people tend to overlook certain aspects of performance management. Apart from its being engaging and comprehensible, I hope this book will be a successful knowledge transfer of such overlooked aspects of performance management.

Acknowledgments

This book could not have been possible without the assistance of many others. The first person I would like to thank is my wife, because she inspires me to write. She is also one of the first fans of my Facebook fanpage, and is usually the first person to tell me that my morning post was difficult to understand. In addition to her reviews, she also helped consolidate and edit various articles, gather many files together, and create and format layouts. In other words, she has been my editor.

Next, I would like to thank my daughter Paan and my son Pun for the moral support, their smiles and laughter...

I am grateful to my parents for their knowledge and support. I also appreciate my younger brother's continuously exchanging thoughts with me.

I thank my research and teaching assistants for gathering the relevant data and works. I am also grateful to Pat Juthamard, who helped me translate the Thai version of this book into English.

In addition, I would like to thank the fans of the *Performance Measurement Fanpage* for their comments, shares, and likes of my daily 7 am posts. These have encouraged me to write this book.

Last but not least, I would like to thank you, the readers.

Table of Contents

Chapter 1 Why measure?

Chapter 2 Benefits of performance measurement

Chapter 3 On measurement

Chapter 4 Cautions of performance measurement

Chapter 5 Get to know the system of performance measurement

Chapter 6 Things you should know before creating a performance measurement system

Chapter 7 Design a performance measurement system

Chapter 8 Create a performance measure

Chapter 9 Set targets and collect data

Chapter 10 Prepare a performance report

Chapter 11 Do not use it if it fails a test

Chapter 12 Implement a performance measurement system

Chapter 13 Put the data from performance measure to good use

Chapter 14 Make your performance management system sustainable

Why this book?

I really love reading... Not only does it promote imagination and is a wonderful kind of entertainment, but it also gives knowledge. A book can change our lives. Looking around, I saw plenty of books lying on the shelves, commonly referred to as "academic" books. I realized that these books contain a lot of knowledge and benefits. Yet, people are not interested in them. Why?

What is the difference between these books, and the ones on the "Best Seller" shelf? The answer is "simplicity" and "engagement." I have written many of those "textbooks," and I made sure to follow the rules and norms: they should be supported by research, refer to academic theories, have learning objectives, and so on.

As a university professor, I followed the format of what universities or public organizations would define as a "textbook", partly to obtain academic positions, as they proved my in-depth academic knowledge. However, these textbooks lacked simplicity and engagement, even though they might have been useful. Completing a textbook is quite a difficult task, as it requires research and crafted writing to express the author's intentions. It is a pity that very few people are actually interested in these textbooks. The readership of these books is usually the students who are studying a particular subject. If that subject is mandatory, then more students will study it. However, if the subject is an elective, less number of students will study it. Most importantly, the student's main objective in reading these textbooks is to memorize the content for exams. On the day after the exam, as one of the textbook writers, I am stabbed in the heart... Those textbooks will be coldheartedly abandoned. Well, if the exam is over, what's the point of keeping them?

Another potential reader group may be working people who seek knowledge about these subjects, but when they walk into a bookstore and read a few pages, they will immediately put the book down. There are many difficult equations and theories crawling all over the pages. They do not understand what is written on those pages. Or if they do, they find it uninteresting, and even after they finish reading, they do not know how to apply the knowledge in real life.

This is what inspires this book. I had once written an academic book called *Organizational Performance Management*, which is used as teaching material for Bachelor's, Master's, and Ph.D. courses. That book was supported by my research. However, I want this textbook to be beneficial to other audiences than just my students. If it comes in the form of a traditional textbook, the general public would hardly pick it up.

With this in mind, I began to write daily articles on the *Performance Measurement Facebook Page* at www.facebook.come/PerformanceMeasurement. There, I try to communicate the knowledge from my textbooks in simple terms, and through interesting real-life examples. I started with a few hundred followers, most of whom were my students. Later on, the number was in the thousands, and shortly after in the ten thousands. As I am writing this chapter, my page has already gathered 60,000 Likes. This proves that something simple and interesting can attract followers. Now, if you are ready, let us begin!

Chapter 1:
Why measure?

Why learn about performance measurement? The first part of this book highlights the main reasons why we need performance management in the first place. Let's see what those are.

#1 Performance measurement helps realize the outcome.

Yes, as simple as that. I think this is one of the main reasons why you should measure. If you do not measure, then you will not be informed, right? Imagine yourself driving... You would check the dashboard to see how fast you are driving, how much gas you have left, and the heat level of your engine. What for? So that you can make a decision. If you are driving too fast, then you will slow down. If you are running out of gas, then you will drive to the nearest gas station. Same goes for business. If you do not measure, you can never know the outcomes of your actions. If you do not know whether or not your customers like your product or service, or how much you can sell, you are literally waiting for the day that you will run out of business.

#2 Performance measurement can be a warning system.

Let's revive the previous example. In addition to providing information on the current status of your car, a car's dashboard also serves as "a warning sign." Normally, I am not an observant person (please do not be like me). I always start the car and drive off without checking the gas. Most of the time, I will suddenly notice the yellow light of the fuel level gauge. This is what I mean by a "warning sign." When the yellow light appears, the driver knows that he has to be careful, because there is not much gas left. The driver would then look for a gas station to fill up the gas tank, because if he keeps on driving, the car would definitely stop moving at one point.

Organizations need measurements like these, because if they just wait to see the final result, such as profit or loss, it might be too late – akin to waiting for the car to stop moving first, and then searching for the reason why the car stopped working. Performance indicators, such as repeat purchases, can serve as "warning signs" for an organization, so they can understand if their strategy is on the right track or not. If customers return, then the strategy should be right. Whereas, a decrease in the repeat purchase rate could be a bad sign, signaling to the organization that its strategy needs to be reviewed and revised before any real damage is done. It can be too late to fix things sometimes.

#3 Performance measurement changes behavior.

The first question is "why change behavior?" For an organization's strategy to be successful, employee behavior should be in alignment with that strategy. Let me give you an example. Assume that the strategy of a company is "to make a difference" The company could never make a difference if its employees think traditionally and cannot innovate. So, what can we do for the employees to be innovative? I see many organizations try to communicate to their employees that it is necessary to think outside the box. They arrange meetings to clarify the matter, make announcements through the company's Intranet, or even through a notice in front of elevators. Is it an efficient way to apply the strategy? I think it is, because employees would gradually absorb the idea. However, if you ask me how long it would take to see the results, I would bet very long. Have you ever read something in front of an elevator and felt like "I need to change the way I work right now"? I think that hardly ever happens.

So, what should we do to make these employees aware of the importance of this matter? The simple answer is to measure everything that is important. If you want your employees to see the importance of innovation, then try to create performance measure metrics, such as "the number of beneficial suggestions", and tie them to incentives. Of course, every employee would want the incentives, and they would realize that in order to receive the rewards, they will need to come up with new ideas and make suggestions to the company. Yes, at first, these behaviors might happen because the employees are being measured and want an incentive, but eventually they become part of a routine, and develop into "the culture" of the company.

#4 Performance measurement translates strategy into action.

During a lecture, I asked the attendees, "Whose organization has a strategy?" Most raised their hands. However, when I asked the next question, "Whose organization can translate everything in their strategy into action?" Raised hands disappeared all of a sudden. This incident does not happen only in a particular country, it happens everywhere. All organizations have strategies, but, most of the time, those strategies are not translated into action. Performance measurement can help, as "you get what you measure." If you want to turn strategy into action, then you have to measure it.

I had asked my students once if they believed that performance measurement could really help translate strategy into action. Most of my undergraduate students had no work experience, so they could not imagine. I asked them if they would be OK with not having to take an exam for my course. Most of them said they would be OK with it. Then, I would tell them that they have to promise me that they will go back and review the material as if they were going to take an exam. Everyone laughed, because they knew by heart that they would not do it. An exam is a kind of performance measurement. If the students do not have to take an exam, then they would not have the motivation to review the lessons. Hence, performance measurement is one of the tools that can translate strategy into action. In addition, it will also give you the results of your action. Therefore, performance measurement is one of the tools that encourages action.

#5 Performance measurement helps monitor trends.

Jeff and James both scored 60. Who do you think had more problems in studying?.. Well, they got the same score, so they should have equivalent problems. Let's think about that again. For the past four weeks, Jeff scored 30, 40, 50, and 60, while James scored 90, 80, 70, and 60. Now, who do you think has more problems? It seems to be James, right? His performance has declined over the period, whereas Jeff's performance has continued to improve. See? Receiving the same score did not mean they both had problems.

Apart from reflecting the current status, performance measurement can also be the tool that informs you about trends. We can use a past trend to predict the future so that we can develop a prevention plan. So, is your organization Jeff or James?

#6 Performance measurement helps allocate resources.

There is a tank full of water with many leaking holes. What should we do? Well, find something to plug those holes with. Yes, that's right. If we can plug all of the holes, water will stop flowing out, and the problem will be solved. But... Life is not that simple. Let's assume that you have a very limited amount of clay that can be used to plug those holes. You cannot plug every hole. So, what should you do? Think about it... If we divide the clay into tinier pieces and try to plug every hole, in the end, it might turn out that we could not stop any leaks, because the pieces of clay were too small for the holes. Plus, we would lose all the clay, and the water would continue to leak from every hole. You can solve the problem in another way by using the limited amount of clay to plug only the few large holes so that you can stop 80-90% of the leaks, and plug the rest of the holes once you have more clay. Even if you do not have the additional clay right now, at least a smaller amount of water will leak. This is a better solution, right?

Same goes for organizations. Every organization has problems, and problems never care if we have enough resources to solve them. And most of the time, problems occur when we have few resources to spare. Using the limited amount of resources to fix all the problems that occur at the same time might not be the best option. Apart from the fact that it might not fix any problem at all, it might even cost us all of the limited resources.

Wouldn't it be better to allocate the limited resources to resolve the most important problem first? Once that problem has been fixed, we might find that we were able to prevent 80-90% of the damage. Once we have more resources, then we could start fixing the rest of the problems. My point is that performance measurement will tell you which problem is the most important and needs your attention first. The less significant problems can be fixed later. Simply put, performance measurement will help you prioritize your problems.

#7 Performance measurement can teach.

Have you ever noticed that we measure different aspects of our projects mostly before we start them, rather than after we finish? Prior to starting a project, we measure everything – profit rate, return rate, breakeven point – even though the numbers obtained from projections have very high uncertainty levels (since most of them are just predictions.) Before we begin a project, we should make predictions to make sure that our project will be worth it, because once a project begins, a lot of money is already at stake, which makes it hard to turn back.

A good project analysis could lead to future success. Have you ever measured the results of your project after you were done, to see whether everything progressed in line with your predictions or not? It is true that you cannot turn back the time, but if you measure your finished project's performance, you can learn from your mistakes, and never make the same mistake twice. George Bernard Shaw, one of the founders of the leading academic institution London School of Economics, had said: "Success does not consist in never making mistakes but in never making the same one a second time."

#8 Performance measurement can be a marketing tool.

Do you believe that organizational performance measurement can be used as a marketing tool? What?! We have always been taught that marketing is just the 4Ps: Product, Price, Place, and Promotion. Isn't that right? How can key performance indicators (KPI) used in measuring organizational performance become a marketing tool?

Here's the thing. Normally, in an organization, we do not use only one KPI, because we have to measure many important factors. Some KPI outcomes might turn out good, and some bad. What turns out bad are the weaknesses of that particular organization. The benefit of knowing the results is that we can work on those weaknesses to resolve or eliminate the problems. On the other hand, aspects with excellent KPI results would reflect our strengths, right? This is where we can utilize KPI as a marketing tool. We usually see advertisements like "100% satisfaction," or "Best Place to Shop," etc. These things that we present to customers might be the results of organizational performance measurement. So, go back and take a look at your organization's KPI to see if there is anything in there you should tell the world about.

#9 Performance measurement is input for incentive systems.

I believe everyone waits for a "bonus" or "reward." We sit on the edge of our seats hoping to get it at least once a year, right? Giving rewards or bonuses to employees is a great motivational factor. Yet, it can also discourage employees, if done incorrectly or unfairly. What is fair? This question is very vital. "Equally shared" does not always mean "fair." Think about what would happen if you give everyone an equal amount of bonus?

The employees who work hard would be discouraged, because those who don't work as hard still get the same amount of bonus. And those who do not work hard would think that what they are doing is good, because even when they do not work, they still get the bonus. Why work at all then? In the end, the organization would only have people who do not want to work. I do not need to tell you what is going to happen to this organization next, right?

Organizational performance measurement is one of the tools that we can use to help make decisions about employee incentives. Of course, we might not be able to use performance measurement to help decide on employee incentives 100%, because each job is different. However, at least the performance that is reflected by KPIs can help us make "better" decisions than those based solely on our judgment. Giving incentives can be hard, and has always been a difficult management task. However, used correctly, KPIs can become motivational tools that lead to continuous improvement.

#10 Performance measurement can be a benchmarking tool.

Let's imagine you are a tennis athlete... Who would you want to train with: the world's number one tennis player, or your high school friend? If you play soccer, which team would you want to play against: the world champion, or a primary school team? The answer for the questions above depend on your objective in competing. If you compete for a chance to win, then you would play tennis with your high school friend, or play soccer with the primary school team. However, if you play to improve, I think most people would choose to play tennis with the world's number one player, and play soccer with the world champion.

Same goes for business. If you want to be better, you need to look up to the ones who are better than you in the aspects that you want to improve. Learning from the better ones is best practice. Instead of having trials and errors all by yourself, you can learn from those who have been successful. This is what we call "benchmarking." No one can be better than you in every aspect; sometimes you are better, and sometimes they are better. Wouldn't it be nice if you can exchange knowledge so that both parties can be successful together. Yet, benchmarking would mean nothing if you do not know what you are good at.

And this is another benefit of organizational performance measurement; it reveals what you are good at, and more importantly, what you are not good at. Performance measurement reflects your weaknesses, which can be used for benchmarking that would eventually lead to the betterment of the organization.

#11 Performance measurement increases motivation.

Who likes to play online games? Whether it is Facebook games, or any other popular online game, there is one thing that makes games addictive. Do you know what that thing is? It is the competition displayed on the leaderboard! The tougher the competition, the more fun it is. What follows is that we will try to win by coming up with different strategies; we will use our free time to play the game, and feel like time has flown by. But, have you ever felt like that when you work? (I doubt I need to wait for an answer.)

Let's take a look at this again. If we work as if we are playing a game, how interesting would our jobs be? When executed well, performance measurement will inspire us to work and develop to achieve set targets. Performance measurement can turn a boring work day into the day we are waiting for, and our Monday mornings might never be the same again.

Chapter 2

Benefits of performance measurement

In the previous chapter, we discussed why we need performance measurement. In this chapter, before we get to learn what performance measurement is, or how it can be done, I want everyone to get a clearer picture of the benefits of performance measurement. Understand the goal before finding a solution... So, if you are ready, let's see what kinds of benefits performance measurement has to offer.

#1 Help monitoring activities

What quality should management possess? A good manager does not need to do everything by himself, without any mistakes. A good manager might not be the person who goes home last, in order to finish every task at hand. Rather, a good manager is someone who can create a team environment where members work is in alignment with the organization's mission.

How can you make your subordinates work the way you want them to? Many people utilize various methods in controlling the way their subordinates work. A control system that requires physical control usually comes at a high cost. For example, if we want our salespersons to actually sell products, instead of traveling around for fun, we might need to measure the distance these people have commuted, and ask our customers, or even ask another employees to follow them around. But this kind of control method requires a lot of investment. Also, employees might get the impression that you do not trust them.

So, what can we do? How can we make sure that our employees do not get sidetracked, or do something that our organization would not approve of? Performance measurement is the key to help solve this problem. If you want to monitor the activities of salespersons, simply measure their sales volume and accordingly provide incentives. As simple as that! Now you can manage the way your salespersons work, and be rest assured that your employees will comply with your organization's goals. This method does not require a lot of investment, and would not make employees feel like management does not have enough confidence in their abilities.

Have you ever wondered why you have to take an exam after you finish a course? I used to wonder that, too, and I believe many people are curious about the same. Yes, exams can demonstrate whether we have acquired the required knowledge of standards or not. Yes, exams can demonstrate who knows more than who. Yes, exams can demonstrate your weaknesses so that you can address them for betterment. However, I think there's even more to exams than that. Examination is a kind of performance measurement. Let's think about it... If there were no exams, how many people would attend classes? How many people would pay attention in class? How many people would review their lessons? What would have been missing are these activities. More importantly, these activities are all beneficial. Examination is a control tool, which, if applied well, yields great benefits. Actually, the result of an exam itself is less beneficial than the activities that students perform in preparation for the exams, such as reading books and reviewing lessons.

#2 Determining your scope of work

Have you ever wondered what your scope of work actually is, and where you can find the relevant details? Many people would say, "Well, just look at the job description." A job description is a good information source on your scope of work and responsibilities. However, the problem is that job descriptions provided by some companies include every task that could possibly exist - pretty much everything under the sun. So, although given the job description, your responsibilities and scope of work might still be unclear. Or sometimes, there are cases when you will only see five tasks in the job description, and think it is not that difficult. However, in reality, you will not be executing any of the tasks 1 to 4, but you will always be working on the 5th one: "other assigned tasks," which simply means that you do whatever your boss asks you to do!

I think that many of you have experienced the above problem before. Having KPI as one of your tools can help solve the problem one way or another, because performance indicators tell us about the main task that we need to achieve. If we tell our salespersons that we are going to measure the "sales volume," it practically implies that we want our salespersons to know that they need to "sell products." If we tell our production manager that we are going to measure "defect rate" and "on time delivery," it is like we are telling our production manager that his or her job is to "produce good quality products and deliver them on time." I think it is possible that sometimes the KPIs that we use, can perform better than unclear job descriptions.

#3 Translating strategy into action

Everyone must have heard of the word "strategy," but few really know what it is. Strategy is what an organization develops to achieve its goal. The basics of strategic management involve planning, implementation, and evaluation. The problem with most organizations is not the lack of strategy, but rather the implementation process.

Many organizations have annual strategy reviews, and have management teams attend a seminar to brainstorm about the best strategy. The problem happens afterwards – when the formulated strategy is not put into action, and rather laid on the shelf. Why isn't strategy always translated into action? I think this problem has many causes. One is that most employees do not know what a strategy is. Even when organizations publicize their strategy through various channels, it does not reach every employee. More importantly, employees might be aware of the strategy, but still not realize its importance. Performance measurement is one of tools that can solve this problem. As strategy is measured, we will need to know what it really means. The terms like 'effectiveness', 'efficiency' or 'sustainabiltiy' will be translated into more operational terms hence managers will understand more clearly and thus strategy can finally be put into action.

#4 Understanding the process

In addition to providing us with the results that can be used to improve the way we work, performance measurement has another benefit that you might not be aware of. Can you guess what it is? When designing indicators or analyzing results, another thing to consider is the business process, which turns strategy into action.

For example, an academic institution has the strategy to produce graduates of distinction for society. Hence, the institution needs a "teaching process" to achieve its goal. We create performance measurement systems to control the processes that will enable us to achieve our goals. When designing any performance measurement system, the question will arise: what is "this process" for?

This question is particularly important, and could lead to process elimination. Some processes might have been necessary in the past, but no longer needed in the present, such as a government policy. However, we still follow that same process because we had done it last year. Performance measurement will make us question, "What is this process for?", which would then lead to future improvement. This is another unexpected benefit of organizational performance measurement.

#5 Knowing your limits

How fast can you run 800 meters? Most people cannot answer this question. The reason is that you have never measured it before, right? Performance measurement makes us see our own limits; we can learn how fast we can run 800 meters, how much weight we can lift, and how far we can jump. Once we know, we can improve. That is why athletes always measure their performance when they are training or competing.

Same goes for organizations. If we do not measure, we would never know how much we can accomplish. If we never measure, we will never improve. Hence, another benefit of organizational performance measurement is that it enables us to become aware of the limit of each process. For example, we can find out how many customers we can serve per day, how many items we can deliver to customers per month, or how fast we can respond to customer complaints. Once you realize that, you will be able to improve your process. Do you know the limits of your own work processes?

#6 Help in betterment

Did you know that, apart from exercising and reducing calorie intake, there is another technique to reduce weight? Weigh yourself every day. It sounds strange – how can weighing yourself make you lose weight? Actually, weighing yourself does not help you lose weight directly, but it does help indirectly, because it will affect you emotionally. Weighing lets us know if we have gained or lost weight. If we weigh more than before, the measurement reminds us to take control of our weight, one way or another. If we weigh less than before, then measurement encourages us to lose weight. Many of you might have noticed that once we stop weighing ourselves for a certain amount of time, then measure again, our weight tends to increase. That is because there was no performance measurement to control us.

Same goes for organizations. Sometimes organizational performance measurement does not have a direct effect on quality or the productivity of employees. However, it imposes an indirect effect by acting as a warning system, or as encouragement for the employees. If the result of performance measurement turns out to be negative, we will be able to get our hands on the problem quickly and solve it. If the result turns out to be positive, then we would be encouraged to move forward. So, we can say that if organizational performance measurement is done well, it can be a tool that encourages improvement and productivity.

#7 Help in prioritizing problems

Have you ever been in a situation where many problems occur at the same time? How did you deal with those problems? Usually there are four kinds of management in terms of the methods with which they deal with problems. Let's see what kinds of management those are.

The first kind is the kind that just sits around, hoping the problems will just go away. This approach might be effective for certain problems. But mostly, it does not work at all. And sometimes, small problems turn into bigger problems, much harder to fix.

The second kind arranges a meeting to solve the problem. Well, it does sound good at first, but the thing is, meetings only convey that we have plenty of problems, and we want everyone to participate in solving them. After we leave the meeting room, no one knows what he or she needs to do. We only point fingers at each other, saying, "It is your responsibility, not mine." This is the kind of organization that deserves a "You Do It" award.

The third kind tries to solve all problems at once. Sounds like the right way to do it. However, there is one problem: limited resources. If we delegate the limited resources to fix all problems at once, in the end, none of the problems might be solved. In addition, we would lose all the resources.

The fourth kind is the one that solves the most recent problem. Do not forget that the most recent problem is not necessarily the most important one that deserves immediate attention. We might even risk losing resources in fixing unimportant problems.

These four kinds of management occur in organizations with poor performance measurement systems, or in those that do not put performance measurement to good use. If there is a complete performance measurement system and the outcomes of the system are utilized, apart from knowing which process has a problem, we would also know which problem should be prioritized. Organizational performance measurement can play a part in prioritizing problems, and help management with resource delegation to correctly solve problems.

#8 Forecasting

Do you want to know the future? Of course, we cannot expect 100% accuracy in forecasting. However, we can estimate. The most popular kind of estimation is to use historical data. We forecast future stock prices based on historical stock prices; we forecast sports scores based on past scores, because we believe the past is a good indicator of the future. Hence, acquiring historical data is very important.

Organizational performance measurement is a tool that provides us with historical data. When we have enough data, we can then utilize that data to forecast the future. Furthermore, organizational performance measurement helps us realize the limit of each working process, which will help us predict the future more accurately. For example, if we know we can serve no more than 100 customers per day, then we would know that our revenues will come from no more than 100 customers per day. So we can say that organizational performance measurement can be used as a tool to forecast operational results, too. Do you want to know your organization's operation results for tomorrow?

#9 Giving you the courage to assign work

Shortly after I graduated, I used to meet up with my college friends. After work, we would frequently have dinner together. After a while, we still had our usual meet-ups, and from time to time, some of my friends were not be available. Generally, everyone usually participated. But one day, one friend of mine disappeared. Every time I called, he would say, "I'm very busy." I heard that this friend had recently been promoted as a "manager." He used to be able to go home at 5 pm every day, but now he goes home at 1 am or 2 am every day. One day, my friends got curious, so we dragged that friend out to dine with us. We asked him as to why he has to go home that late. Doesn't he have any subordinates? The answer was that he does have subordinates, but he does not feel like leaving his work to his subordinates. He was "afraid that his subordinates wouldn't be able to deliver good work" like he does.

This point is very interesting. I believe that many managers are just like this friend of mine. They are not willing to delegate work to other people. And even when they allow other people to do their work, in the end, they end up doing it themselves. Thus, the manager no longer "manages," instead, they "work" for their subordinates. Operational performance measurement is the tool to help managers solve this problem.

The first reason is that performance measurement is an effective control system. When it is available, workers are willing to work their hardest, so the bad output that managers are worried about is unlikely to be produced. Secondly, when a problem occurs, performance measurement will reflect that problem immediately. Thus, managers will be able to recognize the problem right away, and find a way to fix it. Good organizational performance measurement is like a reliable right-hand man who controls work operations for us so that we can have enough time to "manage."

#10 Helping us admit and take responsibility only for the mistakes we are associated with

There is another story I would like to tell you. A CEO of a company received a complaint from a very important customer that his delivery did not arrive on time. Therefore, the CEO called the production manager to complain, and insisted that he needs to speed up production to deliver items to customers on time. One month later, the CEO received complaints again, from the same customer, on the same matter. The CEO was upset, and called the production manager immediately. The manager explained that he is working at full speed. Before the matter got any worse, the manager came up with an idea for the company to create an operational performance measurement. It would measure the time from when a customer order is received until the products are delivered to the customer, process by process – receiving an order, producing, and delivering. One week later, the results showed that the process that took the most time was not production, but delivery, which faced many delays. The one who deserved to be reprimanded and needed improvement was the delivery department, not production.

From this story, you can see that organizational performance measurement helped the production manager keep his job, and also helped identify the real cause of the problem. This is another benefit of organizational performance measurement.

#11 Changing organizational culture

What is organizational culture? It is what people in an organization value and follow, and also what an organization gives importance to and uses as rules of practice – similar to human behaviors. Nowadays, organizational culture is created because it is necessary for the long-term survival of the organization. Organizations with strong cultures have clear operational direction.

Now, let's test that. If I mention the word "innovation," which organizations come to your mind? Is it something along the lines of Apple or Google? That is because these organizations reflect "innovation" through their new products. In order to establish a strong organizational culture, an organization needs to communicate what employees should give importance to. This is where organizational performance measurement can help.

Think about it. If Apple and Google, which are companies that emphasize innovation, have KPIs like the percentage of decrease in expenses and expect it to decrease 5% every year, we would not be able to witness as many new products from these two companies, because R&D would have budget constraints. Creating the wrong performance measurement system can barricade organizational culture.

On the other hand, assume performance measurement is in alignment with organizational culture - for example, if our organization were to promote a culture of innovation, and some of our KPIs were the number of new products or the percentage invested in R&D, employees would pay more attention to innovation until such behavior eventually turns into a strong organizational culture.

#12 Benefits for employees

Organizational performance measurement is not only beneficial for management, but also for employees. Let's take a look at how employees can benefit from organizational performance measurement. The four main benefits for employees are:

1) Employees will know their scope of work, and understand work objectives. Performance measurement can communicate important matters that should be conveyed to employees.

2) Employees can see how their contribution helps the company succeed, and receive recognition by that success. Performance measurement shows us the results, and when results are represented, there will be recognition. No performance measurement, no recognition.

3) Employee evaluations will be more transparent. Performance measurement results can improve the evaluation process, because they reduce bias, and enable more transparent and fair assessments.

4) Employees will be empowered. Performance measurement puts management at ease, because with it, employees will clearly understand the goals. Performance measurement is already a kind of control tool in itself, enabling management to "feel comfortable" in assigning more work. Also, it can give early warnings as problem arise. Hence, management would no longer be afraid to empower their employees, because they would know that if their employees make mistakes, they will receive warnings and can fix the problems early on. Empowered employees will improve how they work and feel more satisfied with their jobs.

Now, you can see how performance measurement benefits both management and employees.

Chapter 3
On measurement

Having discussed the "why" and the "benefits," let's take a look at "what" performance measurement is, and how many kinds of measurement there are. Also, I am going to answer the interesting question, "Can we measure everything in this world?" So, stay tuned.

What is measurement?

Since this book is about "performance measurement," we need to know what "measurement" is first. Can you answer that question? "Measurement" means assigning a numerical scale to the size, value, or other characteristic of a tangible or intangible object. For example, measuring "the number of persons" (tangible) or "satisfaction" (intangible).

Do you know the most important aspect of measurement? Take a minute to think about it. Do not peek below. The most important aspect is "comparison." All measures are relative. Without a reference for comparison, all measures are meaningless numbers.

Let's assume someone tells you that you scored 56 on an exam. Should you be happy about it? You cannot answer that without knowing the full score. That means that you are already looking for a comparison. Now let's assume that the full score is 100. Now, many of you would say that you should be sorry about it because you scored slightly over half. But just wait... What if I can find another comparison value showing that the average score on this exam is 15? Now, did the whole world just get brighter? Well, the score is little more than half, but it is way above average, right? Now, what if I give you another comparison value? The top score is 56. Well, well, that would be you! Do you feel like jumping up and down? See? 56 means a lot when there is a reference point, and this can help in decision making. Hence, we can say that measuring without comparison is almost useless for decision making, right?

Let's get to know different kinds of measurement.

Now that we know the meaning and origin of performance measurement, let's familiarize ourselves with different kinds of performance measurement. There are two kinds of standard measurement:

1) Standardized measurement uses standard scales commonly adopted around the world. For example, we measure length in meters, weight in kilograms, and time in minutes. These scales are internationally accepted. If you measure 1 meter anywhere in the world, the length will be the same. If you measure 1 kilogram in any country, it will weigh the same. If you measure 1 minute anywhere, it will last the same.

This kind of measurement makes comparing easy and clear. We can say for certain that 10 meters is longer than 1 meter, 10 kilograms weigh more than 1 kilogram, and 10 minutes is longer than 1 minute. These facts hold true no matter where you are in the world.

2) Relative measurement does not use standardized scales like the first type. An example is "customer satisfaction." Organizations of the world do not sit and agree in consensus to use the same measurements or questions for customer satisfaction. If we were to do that, I believe many organizations could not reach an agreement, because different organizations have different kinds of customers and highlights. Hence, having standardized measurement in such a case would be difficult and inappropriate.

Therefore, every organization should have its own customer satisfaction measurement; comparisons should be done within the organization itself. For example, comparing last month's level of customer satisfaction with this month's will be meaningful, because we will have used the same instrument. However, we should not compare this type of value across organizations because instruments and questions will be different. It would be "comparing apples and oranges." You just cannot compare them, right?

We can also divide measurement into two more types based on the measurement method:

1) *Direct measurement* is used to measure tangible things, and the outcome of the measurement would be what we want to know, e.g., number of employees.

2) *Indirect measurement* is used to measure intangible things, so we would need to measure their outcomes, e.g., measuring employee morale through absenteeism because we might be assuming that absenteeism is caused by low morale.

Now, many of you might be wondering which type of measurement is the best one. There is no definitive answer to that question. It depends on the situation. For example, you have one water pipe at home, and you want to compare its length to the one your friend in the other country has, to see which one is longer. In this case, the first thing that you would do is to use a standardized measurement, e.g, measure in meters so that you can compare the result. However, if these two pipes are in the same room, you do not even have to measure. You can just simply put them right next to each other to find out which one is longer.

Same goes for business. Ask yourself before you start measuring:

1) What question are you trying to answer?
2) What kind or method of measurement can you use in answering that question?
3) What kind or method of measurement would be the most efficient and reliable?

Ask these questions each time you are about to choose the kind and method of measurement to use.

Can everything in this world be measured?

This question is very intriguing. The answer is "yes and no." It all depends on what you want to measure. If you want to measure with a 100% accuracy that no one can contest, then you cannot measure everything in this world, especially abstractions, such as love, goodness, and loyalty. These things are all abstract, and their definitions might vary from person to person. For example, some people might measure "the level of love" by the number of times people call each other, by the value of the presents they give each other, or the number of times they miss each other. Those measurements cannot reflect "love" with 100% accuracy.

However, such measurements might be useful if the main objective is to acquire data for decision making. For example, if people never call, never give gifts, and never miss each other, then these things would reflect a certain thing, right? In fact, "immeasurable" implies that something cannot be measured directly. However, things can be measured indirectly, meaning we can measure their outcomes. Measurements like the number of calls, the value of presents, or the number of times two people miss each other, are what we believe the outcomes of love to be (and you might be able to recommend better measurements than mine.) These might not be 100% accurate, but somewhat useful in decision making processes.

In the world of business, measuring things that are (or seem to be) "immeasurable" is quite normal. This kind of measurement happens all the time without us noticing it (TV ratings, customer satisfaction surveys, the quality of a movie by the count of awards received). All of these indicators measure abstract things. Hence, we cannot measure directly, but rather indirectly. For example, "popularity" is intangible, so we measure the "viewing rate," or the so-called "TV rating" instead, because we believe that if one likes a TV show, he or she would turn the TV on to watch it.

Rating measurement is simple. One can simply install a measurement box at the representative sample's houses. Once a participant watches a show on a particular channel, this box will collect the data. Rating is the percentage of the sample watching a show at a certain period of time. We believe that high ratings "indicate" the popularity of a particular show. Or, the number of likes or shares would "indicate" the popularity level of a post on a Facebook page.

When we measure what seems to be immeasurable, most of the time, we only use two gauges like "yes" or "no" – yes or no, love or hate – and we count that as measurement. Let's say before we go to see a movie, we want to know if it is good or not. In the old days, we used to look at reviews from two famous reviewers: Roger Ebert and Gene Siskel. At the end of their reviews, they would give the movies a thumbs up or a thumbs down. Thumbs up means that the movie is worth watching. Thumbs down means the movie is not good. This is a very simple kind of measurement. A movie that receives a rating of two thumb-ups meant that both reviewers agreed that it is a good movie, so most people would be interested in that movie (because it did not happen very often.)

Now you can see that performance measurement is not a complicated thing. If you know what it means, then you can use it. Like in the case of movie reviews, even when a movie receives two thumbs-ups, it does not necessarily mean that everyone will like it. But at least, it lets you know that two famous reviewers like the movie, which is useful.

Quantitative measurement vs. qualitative measurement

In addition to categorizing performance measurement by type and process, we can also divide it into two forms:

1) *Quantitative measurements* are mostly direct measurements that do not require much interpretation, such as counting and quantifying.

2) *Qualitative measurements* are mostly indirect measurements that are based on human decisions, such as measuring employee satisfaction.

We can observe examples of both forms of measurement everywhere. For example, they were used during the Olympics. The measurement used in sprinting or broad jump competitions was mainly quantitative; whereas, for gymnastics or diving competitions, measurement was qualitative.

Have you ever noticed that the sports that usually have problems with scoring are the ones that use qualitative measurement, like gymnastics? That is because it requires judges to give scores, which can be biased. However, that does not mean that qualitative measurements are not reliable. We can use different techniques to reduce bias; for example, we can have more than one judge. Once all scores are in, we can cut the highest and the lowest score out to reduce bias, or we can even issue detailed scoring regulations. For example, if a gymnast makes a certain mistake, points might be deducted. These methods can be utilized to reduce bias in qualitative measurement, and provide more accurate results.

Same goes for the world of business. Most of the time, when people say that something is "immeasurable," it means that it cannot be measured directly. If you cannot measure something directly, then the question you should ask is, "What outcome does that task produce?" From there, you can measure the outcome, indirectly. If there is no outcome that can be measured, it means that the thing cannot be measured, which implies that the particular task should not be attempted in the first place, because it does not affect your organization in any way.

Performance measurement development

Having familiarized ourselves with the definition of performance measurement and performance measurement systems, let's now learn about the development of performance measurement before getting into further details. In fact, we might have to rewind to hundreds of years ago, because humans began measuring profit and loss since the establishment of the monetary system. However, to talk about performance measurement for organizational development, we would have to visit some time after World War II, the mass production era.

The notion of that era was to produce large quantities to reduce the cost per unit. Once the cost per unit is reduced, customers are more interested in buying, because they appreciate cheap things. Hence, it should not come as a surprise that one of the most vital organizational performance measurements during that era would be productivity.

Productivity is a performance measure obtained by dividing the output by input. The higher the value, the more likely we are to succeed, because we have used less input to produce a large quantity of output. This performance measure had always been the most important organizational measurement until the 80s, when people began to question whether measuring productivity alone would be enough, because we have to wait until everything is finished to find out the value of productivity. This measure is not that useful, because it cannot fix anything. It is like finding out where a hole is by looking at the rearview mirror of a car that has already fallen into a hole.

Wouldn't it be better if we could find a measurement that can predict the future? This question is the origin of organizational performance measurement as we know it. Sink and Tuttle were one of the first people to write a book about organizational performance measure, called *Planning and Measurement in Your Organization of the Future*. The book inspired the notion of organizational performance measurement.

During the transitioning period of the 1980 - 2000, many organizational performance measurement concepts were introduced: Balanced Scorecard, Six Sigma, Economic Value Added, and Activity-Based Costing. After the year 2000, less organizational performance measurement frameworks were introduced. However, the focus had shifted to putting existing frameworks into use. More organizations had adopted performance measurement, and integrated it into their management systems. Hence, people started to use the term performance "management," instead of performance "measurement".

Today, performance measurement is becoming more significant. It is related to various branches of study, which perceive "performance" in different ways. For example, marketers might understand performance as brand awareness, while production managers would see it as utilization percentage, and financiers as profit. The definition of performance will evolve. And I truly believe that one day the knowledge on organizational performance measurement will be a branch of study itself, and eventually, it will be no less important than finance, marketing, and production.

Chapter 4
Cautions of performance measurement

Performance measurement is quite similar to taking medication. If you take the right medicine, your will be cured. However, taking the wrong medicine might cause other damages to your health, instead of healing you. Even the best medicine has side effects, and so does performance measurement. If you measure it poorly or incorrectly, there will be side effects. And if you do not realize your mistake, sometimes it can become a fiasco. Hence, in this chapter, I would like to tell you about the possible side effects of using the wrong performance measurement method.

#1 Don't use performance measurement to punish.

One thing that we need to comprehend is that the term "performance measurement" itself has a negative connotation. Think about the times when you were a student. A teacher walks in and says, "We have a pop quiz today." How did you feel? I think most students would feel uneasy. Or, at the workplace, your boss walks in and says, "Today I'll assess your performance." The feeling would be common, something along the line of stressful.

The right amount of unease or stress is a good thing, because it motivates us to work harder. However, we should be careful about not being too stressful or anxious, because it will have more negative effects than good. *Hence, we should not associate our organizational performance measurement with punishment, but rather with rewards*. Associating performance measurement with punishment will reinforce negative effects. Although punishment might yield faster results, you might lose more than you gain.

Imagine your boss announcing, from now on, the company will have KPIs, and whoever fails to meet KPIs will be fired. What would happen? Employees might go on strike, or spread rumors that the company wants to downsize. Employees might see KPIs as their enemy, instead of a tool that would improve the organization. Nothing could be worse than turning performance measurement into an enemy of employees. Apart from the fact that there will be no improvement, it might even hurt the organization. So, be careful!

#2 Be careful not to cause stress.

Have you ever read the news about some college student jumping off a building because he or she felt disappointed? Sometimes when you read the details, you just do not want to believe your eyes. The student committed suicide because he or she did not receive an A on an exam, or did not gain 4.0 like she previously did!

I remember a college student being caught cheating on his final examination. At first, I thought he had done so due to his really low midterm exam score; he must have been afraid of getting an F. But it turned out that he had received a really high midterm score, and he cheated on the exam because he was afraid of not being able to get an A. I even made a joke to the students who received low scores: "Well, if it were you guys, I wouldn't have been surprised." However, one of students replied, "I wouldn't cheat on exams, because even if I have a cheat sheet, I would still get an F." My point is that performance measurement might cause stress. We tend to overlook good performers, because we know by heart that they are good, so we think that we do not need to worry about them. In fact, this is what you should be worried about.

When we are stressed out, we try to find a way out. If we choose the good way, then it is alright. However, if we decide to go with the wrong way, it can harm the organization. For example, if you measure salesperson performance by the amount of sales they make, you might forget about the top performing salespersons, and focus on the low performing salespersons instead. But top salespersons can also be stressed out. For example, imagine this top salesperson who is always number one in sales rankings, but this year he is not. "Over-stimulation" usually happens to the best of us, to "over-achievers." When he is afraid that he will no longer be number one, he will try to find a way out. Finding a good way out such as improving his own sales skills is totally fine. However, if he chooses a bad way out, like cheating or stealing a colleague's sale, then you should beware. As such, instead of stimulating improvement, performance measurement might cause unwanted behavior that might harm the organization.

#3 Be careful not to create a culture of excuse.

Another thing you should be cautious about is to not let poor performers stay as they are for a long period of time. The simple reason is that no one wants to be rubbed in the face that they have failed. Even when you do not say it to their face, they might already feel like a failure because they could not reach the goals. So, what would be the consequence? The low performer might try to improve himself. Self-improvement is a desirable outcome of performance measurement.

However, this method might be difficult, and require such effort that some people might not choose it. Rather, they might end up choosing the second, much easier method: making up excuses such as "the performance measurement system is not good," "the goal is too difficult to achieve," or "the resources are too limited." This is the easier way-out than self-improvement, as it requires only words.

If things turn out like this, there will be no improvement. Let's use health checkups as an example. The results show that your cholesterol level is higher than the standard... What should you do?:

1) Start working out, and reduce unhealthy diet to be healthier.
2) Blame that the cholesterol test is bad, or the standard is too low, and continue to live your life as is.

I believe most people would choose number 1, but in the workplace, we might observe many people choosing number 2. Sometimes, measurements might be flawed, and deserve rectification. If the performance measurement is really flawed, then we should improve the system. However, if this is just an excuse, then we should pay attention to the problem. We should not blame the person, but rather we should help those who could not reach the goal. I believe that most people do not fail intentionally, rather, they fail because of certain problems. Performance measurement will help identify these problems so that everyone can work together to fix the problems to improve the organization.

#4 Be careful not to let the goal become the ceiling.

Goal setting comes along with performance measurement. A good goal can motivate people to work. In contrast, an inappropriate goal will not only discourage your employees, but also become an operation ceiling. What does operation ceiling mean? Here's an example. If you set an easy goal, then once your employees have achieved that goal, they will no longer be motivated. For example, you tell your salespersons that if they can achieve one hundred thousand dollars of sales revenue, you will take them on a trip to Europe. However, it turns out that the sales revenue reached one hundred thousand dollars in June. What do you think would happen next? Of course, salespersons will not be motivated for the next 6 months, because the revenue goal is too low that it has become a ceiling. If you continue like this, you will lose more salespersons. You might also end up losing your top performing salespersons (otherwise they would not be able to achieve the goal this fast). Therefore, you have to be cautious when setting a goal.

#5 Beware of delayed results.

What do you expect to gain from performance measurement? Many people would say "good results." Well, that is correct. But what if the results turn out to be bad? For example, if you know you did poorly on an exam, would you still want to know the result? I bet many would say no. But deep down you do want to know the result, right? No matter how bad it could be, you still want to know, because once you know, you can make decision.

For example, finding out that you scored very low on an exam is still useful, because you will decide whether you should withdraw or try harder to pass the exam. Imagine that you are a freshman, and you have to take an exam for each course. However, the professors never tell you what your grades are, and all you can do is to continue to study. Now, it is your last semester as a senior, and they will tell you all at once: what your GPA is, the list of courses that you passed and failed, and whether or not you managed to graduate. I believe you would feel anxious throughout your college years. Performance measurement makes people who are being measured expect the results. If possible, the results should be delivered fast, and on time.

#6 Beware of perfection.

Performance measurement does not have to be 100% accurate. What?! Why would you say such a strange thing? Performance measurement must be correct. Yes, it has to be correct. But it *does not have to be 100% correct*. Most of the time, perfection requires huge investment, and 100% accuracy is just not worth such huge investment.

Let me give you an example. Let's say we want to measure customer satisfaction by using a 5-scale survey, where 1 = very dissatisfied, and 5 = very satisfied. Let's assume that we had measured customer satisfaction last month as 3.5, and for this month we got 4. Now someone tell us that our current customer satisfaction measurement is not detailed enough, and the scale should be smaller. For example, instead of asking 20 questions, we have to ask 200 questions; and instead of using a 1 to 5 scale, we have to use 1 to 10. What does this mean? The most important thing is investment in data collection. Asking 200 questions and using a scale of 1 to 10 would make it nearly impossible to find respondents who would be willing to complete our survey. We would have to pay them to fill out the questionnaire. Hence, data collection would incur more cost. For example, we might need to hire or provide incentives to respondents. If we give each respondent 5 dollars, and we want to collect 400 samples, then we need to invest 2,000 dollars.

What can we get out of this? Many might say that we will get a more accurate result. Yes, it will be more accurate. For example, we would learn that, in fact, last month's customer satisfaction was 3.5234, while this month's is 4.3245 (using scale of 1 to 5 for easier comparison.) Wow, that is more accurate... However, does it really increase the value of the data we have? Last month's score of 3.5 improved to 4 this month (old measurement), compared to 3.5234 and 4.3245 respectively (new measurement). Our interpretation would be nearly the same. We would also get the same implication that customer satisfaction has improved. The only difference is the investment in data collection; the latter incurs 2,000 dollar more.

Such amount of investment might not affect large organizations so much. However, still, if repeated many times, we would lose quite a lot of money. The same amount of investment might have more impact on Small Medium Enterprises (SME). In conclusion, I do not mean that we should collect incorrect data, but rather, that performance measurement does not need to be 100% accurate. Sometimes, 80-90% accuracy is enough, because the comparison is more important than the actual number.

#7 Beware of depending solely on quantitative measurement.

Many people prefer quantitative measurement that shows numbers or amounts of money, because it is clear. Whereas, qualitative measurement relies on human judgment, and many people don't like it. In fact, measuring by human judgment is nothing new; it is called subjective measurement. Most people are unsure about using subjective measurement, because its results can be contested since people might have different points of view.

For objective measurements, such as the number of employees, the result will always be the same; no matter who measures it, we will get the same number of employees as a result (unless, of course, someone miscalculates.) Whereas, for subjective measurements like employee satisfaction, can easily be challenged. Although the average employee satisfaction index is high, many people might think that it does not reflect overall employee satisfaction. Well, that might be true. When measuring intangible things, we have to admit that we will not be able to find a performance measure or measurement method that would provide us with true values that cannot be challenged. The more important question is, "Can we put measurement to good use, despite it not being 100% accurate?"

For example, if we observe that certain aspects of employee satisfaction has been decreasing, can we utilize that data? The answer is yes, we can. I believe that even though measurement based on human judgment might not be 100% accurate, it is still more useful than not measuring anything at all. In fact, this kind of measurement has not been recently invented. Businesses have been using it for a really long time, and many organizations achieved success due to their implementing this kind of measurement. Performance measurement will always be of use, one way or another.

#8 Beware of incorrect measurement.

How can you know whether your current organizational performance measurement is effective or not? I think this is a very interesting question. Usually, we would consider two dimensions to determine the effectiveness of our organizational performance measurement.

The first dimension is validity. Are the things that we measure and the things that we want to know one and the same? For example, I want to know my weight, and I'm using a ruler to measure my height instead. This measurement has no validity, because the result will be a value of height instead of the weight that we wanted to know. Some of you might think, "But who would do that in the world of business?" Well, let me give you an example from the business perspective. Let's say we want to know about our customer loyalty, what should we measure? Most people would measure "repurchase rate." It is true that loyal customers would repurchase our products; however, customers who repurchase are not always loyal. Why not? Because repurchase derives from many reasons, such as convenience.

I am a frequent customer of a certain bank, because there is a branch near my workplace. But I am not that loyal to this bank, because I know for certain that if this branch moves elsewhere and there is a branch of another bank to replace it, I would immediately switch. Hence, measuring customer loyalty solely with repurchase rate still has a validity problem. Besides repurchase rate, we should also measure recommendation rate or other things to increase measurement accuracy.

The other dimension is reliability. If you use the same measurement multiple times during the same period, you should get similar results. If results are similar, it means reliability is high. If not, then that measurement has low reliability. For example, I believe everyone can rank three of their best friends from the closest to the least closest. If I ask you to do it once more, the result would still be the same. This means the reliability is high. However, if I ask you to rank 100 of your closest friends, I might get a list of 100 names the first time. If I ask you to do it again, do you think the list will be the same? I think not. This is what we call low reliability.

Validity and reliability are both very significant to performance measurement. If you want to measure, then measure right. Am I right?

Chapter 5
Get to know the system of performance measurement

In the first four chapters, I have discussed the reasons behind using performance measurement, its benefits, origin, and cautions. Now, I want to introduce the "system" of performance measurement. Let's see what the system looks like and what it is used for.

Let's get to know the system of performance measurement.

Before we dive into designing performance measurement systems, let's familiarize ourselves with "organizational performance measurement systems" first. Organizational performance measurement system is a management tool, composed of two main parts:

1) Organizational performance measures
2) Supporting infrastructure

This is where things get more interesting. Many of you might think of only the performance measures, aka. KPIs, when talking about organizational performance measurement systems. Performance measures are vital parts of organizational performance measurement systems. However, you should never ignore the fact that the system also consists of a supporting infrastructure. There are two main supporting infrastructures: the data collection system and the reporting system.

Sometimes you might see a failed organizational performance measurement system that is not a product of poor performance measures, but rather an erroneous supporting infrastructure, such as incorrect data or poorly prepared reports. Knowing the definition of an organizational performance measurement system, we would know how to fix the problem at its cause, which will help improving organization management.

What are performance measurement systems used for?

For the most part, a performance measurement system is a tool that helps the management of an organization. Then the question is what are the main responsibilities of management? There are three. The first is to formulate a long-term plan, aka. a strategy. Next one is to deal with day-to-day operation problems, because everything does not simply go 100% according to plan. Hence, "problems" occur, and it is the management's job to deal with them. The last one is to improve work processes. Just because there is no current problem, it does not mean that management can stop working, as management should continue to improve work processes. See? Being a manager is not a simple task. This is why managers deserve assistants to help accomplish their tasks. Let's move on to the next topic and see how performance measurement systems can help management accomplish different tasks.

Devise a strategy to create results.

As mentioned earlier, one of the main responsibilities of management is to create a strategy. Devising a strategy requires two important procedures:

1) Setting long-term goals and implementing intentions, and

2) Making sure every employee understands the goals and is willing to work hard to achieve them.

Generally, organizations have a vision, mission, and values. These three things are an organization's compass.

Vision tells us what an organization would like to accomplish in the long-run. I would like to use a large global company like Coca-Cola as an example. Coca-Cola's vision is based on six important pillars: people, portfolio, partners, planet, profit, and productivity.

Mission answers the question as to why an organization exists. Why has the organization been established? Coca-Cola answers this question simply with three sentences: to refresh the world, to inspire moments of optimism and happiness, and to create value and make a difference.

Organizational value are the principles that guide an organization's conduct, because the organization believes that these principles will play an important role in the long-term survival of the organization. Simply put, values make up the personality of the organization. Coca-Cola's values consist of seven aspects: leadership, collaboration, integrity, accountability, passion, diversity, and quality.

You can see that every global organization has a clear vision, mission, and value. Once an organization has a vision, mission, and value, it must transform these three things into something tangible. And that establishes the organization's main objectives. In the end, these objectives will be translated into operational activities. One of the most vital things in transforming strategy into practice is to establish "business processes." But what exactly are "business processes"? It is a defined sequence of actions that would help an organization achieve its predefined objectives.

For example, a university aims to produce goodhearted graduates for the society. If the university sets the objective but does nothing about it, then of course it would not be able to produce goodhearted and skilled graduates for the society. Thus, the university has to define a certain business process, and that process is teaching and learning. Therefore, we can say that an organization is a consolidation of various processes. How can we push these processes forward and achieve the predefined objectives? This is where operational performance measurement will come in handy with the simple principle of "you get what you measure."

If you want to develop a business process the way you want, then you have to create a control system. However, using physical control would incur higher costs. Let's revisit the previous example. How can you be sure that the teaching and learning process designed by the university will produce goodhearted and skilled graduates? If you rely on physical control, for example, you hire a person to listen to the instructors and observe the students, and have them report on the process. You would have to invest a huge amount of money in hiring a lot of these people. Also, both the instructors and the students would feel uncomfortable with this method.

However, if there is no control at all, there is a risk of instructors skipping classes or not teaching their best, and the students not paying attention (because there is no performance measurement.) In the end, this process would fail. But if a good performance measurement is in place, such as a way for the students to assess their instructor on whether he or she is good at teaching and works hard or not, then the instructors would not be able to neglect their duties. The instructor has to assess the students as well through examination - this way students will pay attention in class. Such teaching and learning process will prevail, because it can create goodhearted and skilled graduates.

Therefore, operational performance measurement is one of the tools that can help manage an organization. When good business processes are predefined, the strategy will be effective. Now let's see what we can measure in order to control the processes. Normally, we would measure input, process, and output. Let's use the manufacturing process as an example. Input measures are as follows:

- Measure input quantity; for example, the quantity of raw materials used in production
- Measure the quality of input materials; for example, the quality of raw materials
- Measure the quality of input procedural quality; for example, the timeliness of raw materials delivery
- Measure other environmental factors related to input; for example, price of raw materials (these are the things we cannot control but have an effect on the organization)

Process measures are as follows:
- Measure the amount of resources used; for example, the resources used in production, or the machine power or labor used in production

- Measure the losses as a result of the process; for example, the defect rate

Output measures are as follows:
- Measure outcomes; for example, the quantity of finished goods
- Measure the quality of outcomes; for example, the quality of finished goods
- Measure the quality of output process; for example, the timeliness of product delivery to customers
- Measure productivity which is an economic measure of output per unit of input

These measures will control and ensure that the procedures would work smoothly. If a problem occurs, you would be informed and be able to deal with it right away, which would then lead to organizational success.

Help in day-to-day operations

Apart from devising a strategy, what else do managers do in their lives? Asking a question like this is asking for trouble. But I do not mean it that way. On the contrary, I asked that question as a lead-in to the main responsibility of management and to the how-tos of putting performance measurement to use. Managers do not spend their time only on formulating a strategy or creating a long-term vision. They also have to oversee and ensure that everything is operating effectively and efficiently.

For example, in production control, managers need to make sure that production runs smoothly, without any problems. But how can a manager know what's going on in production?

Performance measurement is the tool that will help the manager find out whether everything is running smoothly or not. With performance measurement, managers do not need to gather information from various sources, which is time consuming. In addition, when performance measures indicate a problem, such as a decline in the timeliness of production, managers will be immediately notified of the problem so that they are able to fix it on time. Many performance measures might even demonstrate the roots of the problems. Generally speaking, organizational performance measurement is the manager's right-hand man, as long as the system implemented is correct and relevant.

Help in organizational development

Besides working on long-term plans and preparing daily reports, managers have to improve and develop current business processes. Many managers think "Solving daily problems takes the whole day. How can I have enough time to improve procedures?" The catch is you are spending time to fix daily problems because you did not try to improve your process in the first place.

For example, if you never care to improve your production and leave the machines broken, you would feel anxious that you will not be able to produce good quality products or produce goods on time. You have to spend your day seeking for products from somewhere else to be delivered to customers. Taking a step back to improve the process will definitely be worth your time. To develop a better process, you have to work harder only once. After that, you might find that you have more time to work. Performance measurement will show you what you need to improve, so that you can solve the root cause of the problem.

However, I have to admit that performance measurement is rarely used for this purpose. Performance measurement for organizational improvements is like getting a health checkup. You do not get a checkup because you are sick, you get it because you are afraid of getting sick, right? If the result shows that you have certain problems, like high level of cholesterol, you will start to improve yourself by exercising more or eating a healthy diet. Organizations need checkups, too. Have you checked the health of your organization yet?

Chapter 6

Things you should know before creating a performance measurement system

If you have made it to this chapter, by now, you probably want to know how you can design a good performance measurement system. Wait a little longer, do not rush it. Before you can design a good system, you need to know what a "good" system is first. It is like when you want to design a house. Before you start designing, you have to know what your ideal house is like. So, let's take a look at the important factors that you need to know before designing a performance measurement system.

#1 A performance measurement system must eliminate existing problems without creating new ones.

I have a story to tell you. A company has a problem delivering its products to customers on time. To fix this problem, they create a performance measure: the percentage of late delivery. This performance measure divides the number of products that could not be delivered on time by total production. If a customer orders 100 pieces, they produce exactly 100 pieces. However, only 80 pieces are delivered on time, and not the other 20. Hence, the percentage of late delivery equals $20/100 = 20\%$. The CEO aims to reduce the percentage of late delivery to less than 5% within a month. If this goal is achieved, then he will give out rewards. One month later, it turns out that the percentage of late delivery is reduced to 2%. However, the company still receives complaints from their customers about late delivery.

What happened? The company still could not deliver the products of the same quantity on time even though the percentage of late delivery decreased? Why? Let's stop here and take two minutes to think about it.

The answer is that the employees tried improving the percentage of late delivery, however, such action was not in alignment with what the organization wants. Do you know what they did? Let's take a look at the calculation again. The number of products that could not be delivered on time is divided by *total production*. Hence, there are two ways to reduce the percentage: (1) Reduce the numerator (the number of products that could not be delivered on time), or (2) Increase the denominator (total production).

Which one do you think is harder? The employees of this company chose option 2, because option 1 demands hard work. Whereas, with option 2, they only need to produce more than what the customer orders. In this case, they produced more than needed. For example, when the customer ordered 100 pieces, they produced 1,000 pieces. And since they did not rush production, they could manage to produce only 80 pieces on time, while the other 20 were still delayed. Yet, the percentage of late delivery was reduced because the value of parameters in the equation have changed: $20/1,000 = 2\%$, instead of $20/100 = 20\%$.

This kind of problem occurs because the performance measure creator does not pay attention to the overall picture, and creates additional problems like over production. So how can we fix the late delivery problem in this case?

The first method is to adjust the performance measure so that it is aligned with what we intend to measure. Using the above example, we can calculate the percentage of late delivery by dividing the number of products that could not be delivered on time by *the number of products the customer ordered*, instead of total production. With this formula, even if the employees produce more, the performance measure will not be affected. The only way out for them to reduce late delivery would be to produce and deliver faster.

The second method is to involve other performance measures. For example, we can include an inventory level measure, so that when the employees overproduce in order to improve the late delivery percentage, the inventory level will also increase. When other performance measures are included, employees would not dare do what the organization does not desire. In this case, the employees would not overproduce.

The third method is to create a restriction for the performance measure. For example, we want to reduce the percentage of late delivery and *not allow overproduction*. This way, employees will act according to the organization's goals. You can see that designing a performance measure is not an easy task. You have to give careful consideration to it. Otherwise, the performance measure will become the troublemaker.

Let me give you another example. There is a city with ferry service in the United Kingdom. The problem is that the ferry captain receives a fixed salary, so he does not have the motivation to work hard. As a result, customers begin to complain that the captain is not eager to work. Despite having full passengers on board, the captain continues to chit chat, and does not hurry back to pilot the ferry. Once customer complaints reach the ferry service company, management begins to invent a performance measure that would solve this problem. The performance measure they come up with is "the number of trips per day," because they believe this will make the captain work harder. Now, I bet everyone is able to guess what's going to happen next.

Yes, once you count the number of trips, you will get numbers of trips; "You get what you measure." What happens is that the ferry captain does not wait for passengers to board the ferry, because he knows the more "trips" he makes, the more rewards he will receive, and he has to achieve the required number of trips. Hence, waiting for passengers to get on board is a barrier to his goal. So, customers find that now the captain would not wait for anybody. Once he had 3-4 passengers on the ferry, he would leave right away. See how a performance measure that has not been carefully considered can affect an organization very badly? In the end, this company had to adjust their performance measure to be based on the revenues received from the trips so that the goal of the captain and the organization are the same, which is to generate profit.

Let's take a look at another example. This happened in a supermarket somewhere in the United States. The problem with this supermarket was the long waiting line, especially during prime time. The long waiting line problem is nothing new. However, customers were particularly dissatisfied with the sluggish cashiers. As the cashiers were receiving a fixed hourly wage, they did not have to work fast; no matter if they worked fast or slow, they would get the same wage. When the cashiers worked slowly, the customers in line felt dissatisfied because they did not understand why the cashiers would not work faster, given such a long waiting line. Most of the time, the cashiers even chit chatted with each other.

To solve this problem, the supermarket's operation manager set up a performance measure for cashier performance. This performance measure focused on the time a cashier spent in servicing a customer. But the problem was that counting the amount of service time was unfair for the cashiers, because the cashiers that get to serve the customers who buy few items would obviously spend less time, and vice versa. Therefore, measuring by dividing the total service time by the number of purchased items was more rational. The total service time would start when a cashier begins to scan the first item, and end when the cashier scans the last item. Then they were able to divide the total service time by the total number of scanned items. In addition, the management of this supermarket also found the statistical value of the performance measure, and defined a goal of spending less time in scanning an item that rewarded the cashiers.

One week later, the performance measure showed significant improvement; time spent per item was greatly reduced. Technically, the time spent in the waiting line should have gotten shorter, right? However, that was not the case. The time spent in the waiting line got even longer than before. How is that possible when the checkout time per item is reduced? How come did the waiting line get longer?

Here's what happened… The performance measure started measuring when the first item was scanned, and ended when the last item was scanned. It is true that the decreased value reflects the reduced amount of time, when compared to the checkout time of the same quantity of items. However, it does not reflect the total waiting time. Once this performance measure was implemented, the cashiers were under the pressure of having to improve the value (the value had to be reduced). Thus, the cashiers began to take certain actions to reduce this value. However, these actions became the reason why the waiting line got longer.

What did the cashiers do? Firstly, when a customer approached the counter and took items out of her cart, normally the cashier would start scanning the items right away. However, because of this performance measure, they did not do that. They would wait until the customer finished unloading the cart, because they knew that the clock would start ticking when they would begin to scan the first item. The customer's unloading her items very slowly was affecting this performance measure.

Another possible situation in this scenario is when a customer unloads his cart for the cashier to start scanning, but then he realizes that he forgot something. In the past, the cashier would continue to scan the other items while the customer ran to grab the thing he forgot. With this performance measure in place, the cashier would not do that, because whenever he starts scanning, the clock starts ticking. If the customer takes a long time, the cashier's performance measure would indicate that he is doing a bad job. So, we would see cashiers standing and waiting for their customers to come back before starting the scanning process.

Thirdly, what if the customer realizes that he forgot something after the cashier starts scanning? In this case, the cashier would not be able to prevent the customer from going back and grabbing something he wants. But at the same time, the cashier cannot stop scanning, so he has to continue what he's doing. But what might happen is that once the cashier finishes scanning, he might finish the transaction without waiting for the customer to return, not to prolong his total transaction time. Despite the fact that he might see the customer already walking back, he would still finish the transaction to stop the clock, and then start a new transaction once the customer is back at the counter. Finishing the previous transaction means that the customer has to pay and sign his credit card for that transaction before the cashier can start scanning again for the new transaction. Therefore, the waiting time would be longer.

Now you can see that designing a performance measure is not an easy job. It is true that in order to reduce waiting times, many actions have to be taken – from increasing the number of checkout counters to other matters. But what I am trying to say is that if you design a performance measure without considering other factors, the performance measure can create new problems without you even realizing it.

#2 A performance measurement system must explain the performance gap.

Once you have received your organization's performance measurement results, you must ensure that you know what the result means. And more importantly, you need to know how you can improve it. Normally, you would receive two values from any performance measure. The first value is the actual value, and the second one is the expected value. Most of the time, these two values are different. You might find that the actual value does not equal the expected (or target) value. The gap between the actual value and the expected value is called the "performance gap." It is very important that you should be able to explain the performance gap once you have a performance measure in place.

Let me give you an example. Assume that we have a measure called "the time wasted without creating added value to production." Of course, we would want the value to be zero (expected value). However, once we receive the results, we realize that we have wasted 100 hours without creating any additional value. The performance gap in this case is 100 hours, or simply put, there is a 100-hour difference from the desired value. Just reporting the 100 hours would be meaningless for the workers, because they would only know that they have wasted 100 hours without knowing any of the reasons behind it.

Hence, a good operational report should contain useful information that can be utilized in problem solving or further development. Therefore, being able to explain the difference is very vital. However, it is not necessary to explain the difference 100% accuracy; 80-90% would do for a start, and later on we can try to achieve about 95%.

From the aforementioned example, apart from being able to tell the amount of time wasted, we can also tell that out of those 100 hours, 50 hours were caused by a broken machine, 30 hours by human error, and 15 hours by the late delivery of raw materials. Now we can use the result to solve problems. It is much better than only knowing that we have lost 100 hours, am I right?

#3 A performance measurement system must include sufficient data.

You cannot start your car, so you take it to an auto shop. A technician tells you that if you let him overhaul your car, he can guarantee that the car will be able to start. Well, that would leave you with empty pockets. A technician should rather inspect your car in detail, and identify which systems or parts don't perform well, and fix those. That would be a wise move costing much less than overhauling your car. This problem occurs when your performance measure is not specific enough. If you only measure input and output, and nothing in between, you will not know the cause of the problem.

Another example… We have two products, Product A and B, but we measure the total sales instead of breaking it down to sales of A or B. What could happen? You might see that the total sales might be stable across time. Looking at the stable total performance, most people would assume that the sales of both Product A and B are stable. Yes, it is possible that the performance of A and B are both unchanged, explaining the total performance's remaining constant. However, that might not always be the case. It is also possible that A's sales is declining, while B's is improving. Yet, when the sales of the two are added up, total sales appears to be constant.

Same goes for stock market indices. When indices remain constant, it does not mean that the stock price of every company in the market remains constant. It is possible that the prices of half of the stocks have increased, while the other half have decreased. Therefore, we can conclude that performance measures that are not detailed enough might hide both opportunities (like the increase in sales of B) and threats (like the decrease in sales of A). As a result, the organization might miss out on many things.

#4 A performance measurement system must be timely.

Can you remember what you had for dinner yesterday? I think most people would remember. Let me ask you another question. What did you have for dinner 15 days ago? Can you remember? Most people would not be able to remember, unless it was a special occasion like your birthday or the day your boyfriend or girlfriend broke up with you. Why can't you remember? I don't even have to ask. Who would be able to remember that long ago?

Reporting the results of our performance measures too late reduces their value, because we cannot remember what had been happening during that time. Think about it... We get the three-month old value of the percentage of defects, and we notice that it is higher than usual. Would you be able to remember what was happening three months ago? Our memory is limited. If we cannot remember what happened, how can we solve the problem?

To make matters worse, if we only realize the problem of three months ago just now, we have no idea how much damage was done during the past three months. This is why I usually compare performance measures to fruits and vegetables. They can be rotten or expired. If we report the results too late, they might be useless. Now is the time for the important question. What is considered "timely" in today's business world? There is no clear answer to that. But I can give you a brief answer.

Measuring weekly should enable us to send out reports within the first days of the coming week. Or, if we measure daily, we should be able to deliver a report by tomorrow. This is what would be called "timely" in today's business world.

#5 It takes time to see the results of a performance measurement system.

Have you ever faced a problem in analyzing the results of an organizational performance measure? Apart from being able to tell if the result is better or worse, we should also be able to tell what makes it that way. For rational analysis, we should look at the changes in other performance measures as well. For example, this month's customer satisfaction has declined. But why has it declined? If we observe other performance measures like the rate of timely delivery, we might find that the rate has decreased. Then we'd know that the decrease in customer satisfaction is caused by the declining rate of timely delivery. This would be an easy case to analyze. However, sometimes analysis could be difficult, because it involves a period of time. What does a period of time have to do with this? Let me give you another example.

Let's assume that our sales performance measure is constant or decreasing. But when we look at other performance measures, we notice that the advertising expenses have increased. Well, that is puzzling. How can an increase in advertising expenses make sales decrease? It does not make much sense, right? In fact, drawing a conclusion like this would be inappropriate, because we did not consider the period of time it would take for advertising to create an effect on sales. "A period of time" starts when we begin to adjust our operations, and ends when an effect is observed throughout a performance measure "learning cycle."

Let's use the same example again. The advertisement that we paid for might require more than a day or two for it to affect sales. It might even take a month. Therefore, if you find that your recently launched advertisement campaign does not affect sales the next day, do not panic. It requires more time. Thus, you should be aware of the "period of time" when analyzing the results of performance measures. Simply put, we need to know or estimate the learning cycle of each performance measure; otherwise, we might make wrong decisions. In the case of the above example, if we rush things, we might decide to cancel the advertisement campaign and start to work on something else without knowing if the advertisement was actually working or not.

The last concern is what to do about performance measures that have a long learning cycle. We might end up wasting a lot of money before we find out if they work or not. Let's use the same example again. Assume that the learning cycle of the performance measures for advertisement is one month. Do we have to air the advertisement for one month? If the learning cycle is very long, you do not have to wait. If you want to measure using sales, then you might have to wait a month. But if you are unsure whether the advertisement works or not, you can try using other performance measures that have shorter learning cycles. For example, you can measure the number of views of that advertisement – you should get the result within a week. If we have already advertised for a week, but no one has seen our advertisement, then you do not have to wait one month to know for sure that it will not stimulate sales. This is just an example.

You can see that if we really pay attention to our performance measures, they actually have plenty of uses.

#6 Performance measurement requires consistency.

When should we use organizational performance measurement?

1) When an organization has problems
2) When an organization does not have any problems

That is worth thinking about. Most of the time number one is the case. For example, you could not deliver goods in time, so you begin to design a performance measure of late delivery to solve the problem. Or, there is a problem with production, and you create a performance measure of defects to deal with the problem. Some people might argue that their organization never has any problems, until they start to use performance measures, and the performance measures become the troublemaker. Sometimes that is the case.

The answer to the above question is "all of the above." Business processes in organizations are like machines – the processes are repeated over and over. For example, you produce goods and deliver them to customers, and collect the money every day. When you stop doing it, it is like you have stopped doing business. Hence, in order for the processes to operate smoothly, we need to control them. Therefore, performance measurement is a necessary tool. But the problem is that many people only use performance measurement to solve problems. Once the problems have been fixed, they stop using that performance measure. A risky action...

Let me give you an example. Let's assume that we have a problem with production. We are producing a lot of defects. One solution is to create a performance measure for measuring the percentage of defects so that we become aware of the problem and find a way to solve it. Yet, once the problem is solved, we stop using that performance measure. You can guess what is going to happen next, right? The performance measure is no longer in place, we lose control, and eventually the problem resurfaces. Many people would say, "Then, reinstall the performance measure." Yes, you can start measuring again, and the problem will be solved again. But if you stop measuring again, in the end, the same problem will return. Can you guess what would happen if this persists? Performance measurement would eventually lose its importance. Even if you start measuring again, the problem will not be solved. Why? Everyone knows that you will stop measuring soon, as you always do. It is akin to developing drug resistance. That is why I always emphasize that you should always measure what's important. Inconsistent measurement includes not only data collection, but also data analysis, data presentation, and implementation.

#7 A performance measurement system must produce comparable results.

As mentioned earlier, *what's more important than the outcome value of performance measures is their comparability*. It is very difficult to make good use of outcomes if they cannot be compared. Outcomes that are hard to compare can cause confusion. For example, if we design "number of defects" as a performance measure, and find that the "number of defects" has increased from 100 last month to 200 pieces this month. It seems like the number of defects is much higher. Also it looks like our production process is deteriorating. Maybe yes, maybe not. The higher number of defects might not be caused only by the poor production process, it might also be a result of more production. The more you produce, the more defects there will be.

Let's say that last month we only produced 1,000 units, and had 100 defects. However, this month, we have 200 defects, and produced 10,000 units of goods. Now we can see that the higher number of defects is not a result of a low quality production process, but of higher production. If we take a look at the "defect rate" instead, it was reduced from 10% (100/1,000) to only 2% (200/10,000). In fact, our production has improved. This is why we usually create performance measures in ratios or percentages, which is easier to compare than unit-counts. Be careful when you use unit-counting performance measures, such as the number of employees who resigned, the number of defects, etc. to avoid problems like this.

#8 A performance measurement system must not cause unnecessary fear.

Most organizational performance measurement system problems are "human" problems. Designing an appropriate performance measure, and considering various relevant factors before creating the measure are both very vital. However, despite flawless performance measures, problems can still occur if user attitudes have not been adjusted.

The term "performance measurement" itself makes people feel uncomfortable. Imagine you are still a student. You probably would not like these words: "There's an exam today," "We're going to have a quiz before class is dismissed," "I'll assign you a project to measure your performance." These expressions can cause stress. Same goes for work; we would feel the same way. "If you cannot achieve this KPI, you will be punished."

These words often create fear and stress, which raises the risk of undesirable employee behavior, e.g., protesting against all kinds of changes. Sometimes these fears become the source of false rumors in the organization, such as "they are going to use KPIs to fire us," "these KPIs are aimed at reducing our salaries." These rumors can become a barrier to organizational improvement. Hence, we should deal with these fears before they create problems. Fears related to performance measurement result from two main reasons:

1) Afraid of being punished, scolded at, embarrassed, etc.
2) Afraid of colleagues getting punished, fired, etc.

Number 1 and 2 can be equally damaging. Therefore, managers have to be aware of these fears if they plan to implement performance measurement in their organizations. Fears should be dealt with the right way. Before putting performance management to use, management needs to inform employees regarding the rationale and benefits of performance measurement. More importantly, they should not use performance measurement as a tool to punish their employees. The enemy of performance measurement is the organization's problems, not its employees.

#9 A performance measurement system must not create the "you do it" culture.

Have you ever heard of a "you do it" organization? A "you do it" culture implies that employees refuse to do their jobs. This usually is the cause of failed performance measurement, because no one wants to be responsible for anything. But who should take care of performance measurement? "Accountability" is a simple principle; the person who is responsible takes both the compliments and the blame. Thus, performance measures should be controlled by an accountable person.

For example, who should be accountable for measuring defects? First, we should ask ourselves who has the power to control and reduce defects. The answer is the production department, right? Then the production department should be accountable for this performance measure.

I have another suggestion about how to select the accountable persons. For the best result, you should assign only one person or one department to be accountable for a particular performance measure. The more people involved, the less accountable a person involved will be. In other words, 'we are accountable' actually means 'no one is accountable'.

Have you ever noticed that none of the organizational performance measures receives enough attention? This is because everyone assumes that there will be a person who is already working on it. So go back and take a look at your organization's current performance measures, and ask this simple question: "Who is accountable for this performance measure?"

#10 A performance measurement system must be correct.

What does it take for an organizational performance measurement system to be considered as a failure? Many would respond, the system would be considered a failure if the organization generates less revenue, incurs losses, or even goes bankrupt. Well, it does not have to be that bad. We can say that a performance measurement system has failed, when the system is not accepted and used. This is already considered as a fail. Normally a failed performance measurement system is caused by these main reasons:

1) The users do not understand the measure, or
2) There is a mistake in the system (e.g., measuring the wrong thing)

If number 1 is the case, then the solution is to train the users on what the performance measure is, and how to use it. But if number 2 is the case, then you need to adjust the system. For example, you can design a new performance measure that is more concise and can better solve the problems. Introducing a performance measurement into an organization is like teaching a new language to everyone. We have to inform people as to why they need to learn the language. Also, we need to hire a knowledgeable instructor of that particular language in order for everyone to learn the new language the right way.

The last question is, how can we know that the current performance measurement system will not fail? Well, we can notice from the decrease in inquiries or complaints. However, the best proof that can indicate the success of this system would be seeing everyone benefit from performance measurement in terms of work development.

#11 A performance measurement system must be "simple" and "relevant."

If you want organizational performance measurement to succeed, I have some tips to give you: *make it simple and relevant.* Many organizations invest a lot of money and manpower to design flawless performance measures and excellent databases. However, no one pays much attention to these measures. In the end, the performance measurement system fails.

The most common mistake is not making sure that the users understand and feel that the performance measures put in place and the data they produce is relevant. Otherwise, no matter how good the performance measure, or how precise the data might be, no one will utilize it. "Simple" means that we have to create a performance measure that is easy to understand. Avoid jargons, and use familiar words that are already a part of the culture. Good performance measures would not raise questions like "What is it?" In cases where you cannot avoid jargons, you must explain the language to its potential users. Do not assume that they would ask if they do not understand. Most of the time, they will not ask, because they do not want to look less knowledgable (why didn't they know such a simple thing?), or maybe they are just simply too lazy to ask.

Another tip is to be "relevant." Everyone wants relevant information, right? A simple example would be Facebook, because Facebook provides tailored information. Your Facebook page is different from other people's. And your friend's Facebook is also different from other friends'. Yet, everyone still receives information from friends and acquaintances. This is what makes Facebook world famous. Sending a report of performance measures to other people is no different. First, you have to ask yourself if the report is relevant to them. Marketing department would want information regarding sales, more than the percentage of defects. If we send the percentage of defects to the marketing department, it is very likely that they would not use the data.

I have a simple rule that you can use to test the effectiveness and efficiency of your report. A good report should make readers understand the main contents in 10 minutes. If it takes longer, it is very likely that they would not utilize the data, which might indicate that the data is not "simple" or "relevant" enough.

Chapter 7
Design a performance measurement system

Time flies... You've already read six chapters. Now is the time for the chapter you've been waiting for. How can we design a performance measurement system? Let's learn how many performance measurement designs and processes there are, and you will realize that designing a performance measurement system is not that hard at all.

Let's learn how to design a performance measurement system.

There are three approaches to designing organizational performance measurement system:

1) Top-down approach
2) Bottom-up approach
3) Integrated approach

The "top-down" approach is when executive management designs overall organizational performance measures first, and then performance measures for each department are created. The advantage of this method is that the management is already well-aware of the organizational strategy, hence the designed performance measures would be aligned with the organizational strategy. In addition, the departmental performance measures would also be in alignment with the organizational performance measures since they were all designed by the same person (or the same group of people.) However, the notable weakness of this approach is that the employees would be dissatisfied, because they were not involved in the development process.

The second approach is the "bottom-up" approach. This method allows employees from each department to participate in designing their own performance measures. After that, the designed performance measures are put together to create organizational performance measures. The advantage of this approach is that the employees would believe in the performance measures, because they were the designers. If they still have doubts in their own measures, then I do not know what else can be done... On the other end, the weakness of this method is that it is difficult to consolidate the measures created by different departments, as they have different directions and not relevant to the organizational strategy, most of the time.

The last one is the "combined" approach. It begins by having the executive management design the organizational performance measures, then letting the employees design their own departmental performance measures. However, there needs to be a theme that guides departmental performance measures to be aligned with organizational performance measures. The pros and cons of this approach fall somewhere between the first and the second approaches'.

Now back to the important question, which approach is the best one? The answer is, there is no best one. It all depends on the characteristics of each organization. Take a look at the pros and cons, and you should be able to select the best one for your organization. Still, the most popular approach is the top-down approach as it is the easiest way to ensure that the measures fit the organizational strategy. So, give it a try.

Design a system in four steps

Before I introduce the main steps of designing a system, let's take a look at the definition of "organizational performance measurement system" once again. Organizational performance measurement systems consists of:

1) Performance measure
2) Supporting infrastructure, which is composed of data collection systems and reporting systems

Therefore, creating a performance measurement system requires the creation of both the performance measure and the supporting system. We can conclude that there are four main steps to building a performance measurement system:

1) Determine what to measure and create a performance measure.
2) Set a target value, and set the data collection system.
3) Design a reporting system.
4) Adjust the system before launch.

If all four steps are properly executed, you will have established your organization's performance measurement system. In the next chapter, I will get into details of each step.

Chapter 8

Create a performance measure

The first important step in designing a performance measurement system is specifying what you should measure. This is the step that creates a lot of misunderstandings. The most common one occurs when people brainstorm on what they should measure, and end up with around 100 performance measures, calling them all "KPIs." In fact, the K in KPI is an abbreviation of "Key," which means important. Is it even possible to have more than 100 important things? Let's see how we can select what we have to measure.

"Strategy" comes first.

Another significant factor in designing an organizational performance measurement system is to *understand the organizational strategy*, because the organizational performance measurement will become one of the tools that transforms strategy into action. Therefore, if we do not know what the strategy is, then we would not be able to design a performance measurement system. If you do not know your goals and how to achieve them, of course, you would have no idea how to measure your success rate. Here's an example... Let's assume that an organization uses a strategy of differentiation; the performance measures should be the number of new products, the number of suggestions, and the R&D expenses. Whereas, another organization that emphasizes a low cost strategy, then the performance measures should monitor other things, such as the cost per unit and the number of defects. Different strategies need different performance measures. Therefore, understanding the strategy should be the top priority, before designing an organizational performance measurement system.

Consider stakeholder needs.

Another thing that we should not ignore when creating an organizational performance measurement system is to *study the needs of stakeholders.* Who are the "stakeholders" of the organization? Many people would only think of customers. Yes, customers are stakeholders, however, they are not the only ones. Stakeholders of an organization include the owner, the management, business alliances, employees, financial institutions, business partners, the public sector, as well as the competitors and the society.

Many of you might wonder why competitors are considered as stakeholders. Let's take a closer look at the word "stakeholders." It implies that they must have gained from or lost something to the organization. What do the competitors have to gain or lose? Get it? The customers! If they only take our customers, then they would no longer be our competitors, because we would be running out of business. Or, if we convert their customers, they are no longer our competitors, because they would no longer be in the business. What about the society? How could the society be a stakeholder? Think about it. If we open an oil refinery in a community area, then of course, we would need the community's approval. Otherwise, conflicts can arise. In exchange, we would need to improve the community's standard of living.

As you can see, all stakeholders give to and take from our organization. Here is what is important... To ensure the success of our organization, we need to satisfy the stakeholders; and in turn, we must gain something back from them. Therefore, a successful performance measurement must be created by taking these people and their needs into consideration. We have to study the needs of stakeholders by conducting a focus group or a survey, and figure out how many levels of needs there are. We can divide those needs into three levels: basic quality, performance quality, and excitement quality.

The basic quality concerns what people already expect to have, a must. So, they usually do not express those needs. Despite the fact that they might not have mentioned it, do not conclude that they do not want it. For example, what do you expect the car you are about to purchase to be like in terms of quality? Nobody would say that they want the car to run, because that is the basic quality that every car must have.

The second quality is performance quality. This level of quality is clear-cut, and can be measured. It is the common answers that people give. Let's use the same example again. What do you expect a car to be like? You might say you want a fuel-efficient, powerful, and luxurious car. These are performance qualities.

The highest level of quality is excitement quality. If we do not ask about this quality specifically, we would not get the answer, because most people would not even think of it. For example, what kind of system would you want your car to have, that you cannot find in today's cars? Your answer might be autopilot, hydropower, etc. These things excite us, right? Studying the needs of stakeholders can make us understand their needs and how to satisfy them, so that we can design a more precise performance measure.

Create objectives and critical success factors.

Once we know the organizational strategy and have already studied the needs of stakeholders, we must convert the strategy and stakeholder needs into the organization's main objectives. An organization's main objectives are answers to the question: "what objectives should be achieved for our organization to be successful?" For example, objectives of an organization could be:

1) Generating profit
2) Increasing customer satisfaction
3) Satisfying employees

Setting main objectives will give us a clear direction as to what we want to achieve. After determining our organization's main objectives, we should define our "critical success factor" that will help us achieve those main objectives. For example, if the main objective is to generate profit, then the critical success factor would be to increase the number of branches, or to generate more sales per branch. Simply put, critical success factor is the cause, and the objective is the effect. However, you should create organizational performance measures only for very important objectives, because sub-objectives will emerge by themselves once we have transformed the main objectives into departmental ones.

Designing performance measures

Let's take a look at the main steps of designing organizational performance measures. Mostly, when we talk about organizational performance measurement, we would brainstorm what we should measure. Brainstorming is a must, however, it is not the first step. Generally, the process would start like this:

1) Define business processes, and assign the responsible person in creating the performance measures for each business process.
2) Arrange a performance measure design training session for those responsible individuals (in number 1) to set them off on the right path regarding the processes and performance measures.
3) Brainstorm to identify the appropriate performance measures. Each performance measure must be aligned with the main organizational objectives, as well as the critical success factors.
4) Consolidate all performance measures to establish organizational performance measures.

It does not sound that difficult, right? Creating performance measures might take months, or even years if the organization is large and complex. However, if it is an SME, then these processes can be completed within a few weeks. So, try to adapt these steps to your organization.

Performance measures must be related to each other.

As mentioned earlier, good performance measures must be aligned with an organization's main objectives and critical success factors. But that is not enough. What I want to add is that once you have designed performance measures, you must ensure that they are related to each other. Let me draw a clearer picture. Assume that one of the main objectives is to make employees happy. In order to make employees happy, we might think that we should give them proper benefits. Can you see the rationale behind this? When we offer proper benefits (critical success factor), the employees would be happy (main objective). There can be more than one critical success factor, for example, anything apart from benefits).

Now, how can we create a performance measure that would indicate the happiness of employees, which is the main objective? We might measure employee happiness by an employee satisfaction score that we could gather from surveys. But how can we measure proper benefit, which is the critical success factor? We can measure the percentage of employee benefit expenses. Once we have created performance measures, we can re-check whether the two performance measures are related to each other or not. From the above example, if the percentage of employee benefit expenses has increased, the employee satisfaction score should increase as well. Generally speaking, if it makes sense, that means the performance measures work. However, if it does not make any sense at all, then we should consider switching to a better performance measure.

Quantitative or qualitative performance measures

This matter will concern the types of measurement mentioned earlier. We can divide performance measures into two categories: quantitative and qualitative. Quantitative performance measures can be measured directly without adhering to human judgment (e.g., production time). Whereas, most qualitative performance measures cannot be measured directly, because they usually involve intangible things that require human judgment. This kind of subjective performance measures usually raise questions.

Let me give you a classic example. I believe that many of you might have conducted research, and distributed questionnaires to measure customer satisfaction. If you have not, I believe that you might have completed this kind of survey as a customer. Let's take a look at the scale first. The widely-used scale is 1 to 5, where 1 means the "least" satisfied, and 5 means the "most" satisfied. Then, the researchers would analyze the data, and draw a conclusion on whether the customers are "rather satisfied" or "rather dissatisfied." No one would ask, "What is the difference between 'least satisfied' and 'somewhat dissatisfied'?" Or, "What is the difference between 'most satisfied' and 'somewhat satisfied'?" Think about it... Let's assume that I am a very rigid person who usually gives low scores. My 2 might mean that I am "very satisfied" (because I usually assign 1s). However, my friend is very easygoing. He gives 5s to everyone, unless he is very upset, then he might give 4s. When we conduct a survey, we simply average the scores between these two people; even though someone's 4 might have less value than another's 2.

As you can see, measuring intangible things is not easy at all. In order to reduce bias in performance measurement due to different standards, we should illustrate "an example of a behavior" instead of just saying least or most. In surveys that require very precise results, researchers might specify a behavior corresponding to each scale level. For example, for 5, the most satisfied, the associated behavior might be, "You are so satisfied that you have written a letter to the CEO of the organization to express your satisfaction." When you see this kind of message, you would know that even though you are satisfied with the service, you are still not satisfied enough to write the letter. Then, you will not give a score of 5. For 1, the least satisfied, an example behavior might be suing the company. So, if you are upset with the service but not upset enough to sue the company, then you should not select 1.

This technique can help adjust the standard of each person, because they now understand the meaning of each score. But of course, as long as we are human, bias will continue to exist. We cannot completely eliminate bias, but at least with this technique, we can get a more precise result. The limitation to this method is time constraint, because surveys like this require details and time. In order for the respondents to complete the survey, we might need to give them incentives, which means the investment in data collection would be higher. You have to consider the trade-off between the result and the expenses, to see whether it is worth it or not.

Financial or non-financial performance measures

We can look at performance measures from another perspective, and categorize them into two main categories: financial performance measures and non-financial performance measures. You can tell these two forms apart by looking at the unit of measurement. If the unit is monetary, then it is a financial performance measure. Whereas, if the units are things like the number of defects or the number of complaints, then the performance measure is non-financial. Sometimes it could be both; for example, revenues per employee, where the numerator is financial but the denominator is non-financial.

You do not need to choose which kind of performance measure is better, because both of them are used in reality. Naturally, in for-profit organizations, non-financial performance measures are the leading indicators, while financial performance measures are the lagging indicators. Since we should measure both the leading and the lagging indicators, we need both kinds of performance measures.

Result or process measures

Let's assume that we want to create a performance measure for a salesperson. Which performance measure do you think is more appropriate: the number of sales by that salesperson or the activities of that salesperson that would help generate more sales (e.g., the number of customer visits, the amount of time spent in responding to inquiries or addressing complaints, etc.)? Which one is better?

The problem with the first choice is that sales is difficult to predict, because it is influenced by various factors. For example, the decrease in the number of sales might be caused by poor economic conditions; it might not necessarily imply that the salesperson lacks the necessary skills. And vice versa – an increase in the number of sales might be due to improving economic conditions, and might not necessarily be a result of good sales skills. If this is the case, then why would we use a performance measure that the salesperson cannot control to measure his skills?

Then, maybe the correct choice is the second one. Just you wait... The second one measures the activities that the salesperson performs to generate more sales. This is indeed something that the salesperson can control. However, what an organization wants is sales, not the number of customer visits. If you use this measurement, then the salesperson would visit 3-4 customers per day. What should we do then?

Before I answer this question, let's take a look at the difference between the two performance measures. The first measure is an example of a result performance measure. It emphasizes solely the results, and is very popular in the West, especially in the US. This measure empowers employees to come up with their own processes, and measures only the end-result. If the salespersons say that sales decreased because of the bad economy, the answer they will get is that the effect of economy will compensate each other when the economy gets better. It is a random effect, which means it can be good at one moment and bad the next. So, you do not have to pay attention to it, because it will eventually cancel each other out.

The second kind of performance measure is called process performance measure. It puts emphasis on the process, and is more popular in the East, especially in Japan. The idea behind this performance measure is that one should be measured based on the things under his control. That is what is considered as fair. What if the salespersons follow each process, such as visiting customers frequently, solving problems on time, etc., but sales still decrease because of poor economic conditions? Should we reward the salesperson for the decrease in sales? The answer is yes, because had the salesperson not followed the process, the sales figures might have been even worse. Therefore, the decrease in sales, in fact, helped the organization because the salesperson worked his hardest, and followed each process correctly.

In contrast, if the sales figures of another salesperson increases although he did not follow the process – he did not visit the customers or correct any complaints –, despite the increase in his sales, he does not deserve any rewards, because the increase in sales is not a result of his performance, but of other factors like a recovering economy.

Now let's get back to the question: which one is better? That would depend on the culture and the values of each organization. In reality, we do not have to choose one; we can use both, because each performance measure has its own pros and cons. If we use them together, we can get better results.

Tips for creating effective performance measures

There are a few techniques I would like to introduce. You should consider these eight things if you aim to create good performance measures:
1) Start by studying the main objectives and the critical success factors of your organization.
2) Try to look beyond financial performance measures.
3) Try to find cause and effect relationships between designed performance measures.
4) Include both leading and lagging indicators.
5) Include both quantitative and qualitative performance measures.
6) Consider the possibility of acquiring data and the validity of the created performance measures.
7) Try to acquire information from within and outside the organization.
8) Use simple language and avoid jargon.

Try to include these eight tips in your checklist when you are working on creating performance measures. Or if you already have performance measures, then re-check them considering these tips. If you lack one of them, you can use it to improve your performance measures.

Chapter 9
How to set targets and collect data

There is a saying that goes, "goals are meant to be smashed." But before we can smash them, we need goals first. Now let's see how we can set goals to create results. Once we have the goals, we will take a look at how we can collect data for performance measures. Do not forget, "Garbage In, Garbage Out." If the input is garbage (meaning it is bad), the output will be garbage.

How to set target values

One of the most challenging parts of performance measurement for me is setting target values. After a performance measure is designed, the target value will be the indicator that tells us when we have succeeded. Without target values, we would be walking aimlessly, without a final destination. Thus, setting target values is a very important thing.

So let's talk about the time frame in setting target values. Good target values require time frames. Normally, we would divide target values into two levels (or if you want more levels, it is totally up to you): short-term and long-term. Here is another question without a definite answer: what is considered as short-term or long-term? In fact, it all depends on the industry, and other factors. In the past, when we talked about long-term, mostly it would mean around five years. However, today's long-term is becoming shorter and shorter; most of the time, it would mean around three years. Some companies even consider one year as long-term. All in all, it depends on how fast a particular industry is changing. For now, I will consider three years as long-term in examples. When setting target values, we have to think about where we want to be in the next three years first.

Here is an example so you can get a clearer picture. Our defect ratio is 6,000 ppm (parts per million). How many defects should we have in the next three years ? We can start by benchmarking with our superiors. Now, there might be another question: will they give us any information about their practices? Agreeing on information sharing would be a win-win situation. For example, if they are willing to share certain practices with us, then we would share our good practices with them, which is a possible case. Or sometimes we might benchmark with the companies that are not our competitors. These could be companies that are operating in other countries and have different target customers than ours.

Once you receive the information, do not forget that most of the information will be current. For example, the best of the industry has a current defect ratio of 2,000 ppm. If we want to be number one in the industry, we have to be aware of the fact that the industry leader will continue to improve itself as well. However, it would be harder for them to improve than us, because they are already the best. Let's assume that in the next three years, their defect ratio will be 500 ppm, so we set that value as our target, meaning that our long-term target regarding defects is 500 ppm. This is how one can retrieve a long-term target value. However, many people might raise the question, "Who can I benchmark with if no one is willing to share information with me?" or "I'm already the best in this, it would be hard for me to benchmark with someone else" (You are very confident, aren't you?). Do not panic. If there is no one for you to compare yourself with, you can set up your own targets. You can look at past data, and ask your employees to brainstorm on how much further you can improve in the next three years (long-term target). In the end, you will have your long-term target.

Now let's talk about short-term targets. For example, what should the target be for this year? Let's say our long-term target is to have a 500 ppm defect ratio, but our current ratio is 6,000 ppm. Let's go with the most straightforward method. If your current defect ratio is 6,000 ppm, and in the next three years you want it to be 500 ppm, then the ratio needs to be decreased by 5,500 ppm. Therefore, on (linear) average, we must reduce 5,500/3, or approximately 1,833 ppm, per year. Hence, after the first year, our defect ratio should be $6,000 - 1,833 = 4,167$ ppm, or 4,200 ppm if rounded up.

However, for the ratio to reflect the reality, maybe we need to consider what needs to be improved or developed first. Most of the time, the early stage of improvement is easier than the later stages. If you ever tried to lose weight, you would deeply understand what I am talking about. In the early stage, you can lose 2-3 kilograms only by reducing your calorie intake. But later on, your weight just refuses to decrease, and you have to start exercising. Same goes for performance measures. In the early stage, it would be easy to reduce the defect ratio, because no matter what you lay your hands on, you can simply improve it. But in later stages, it would get more and more difficult, because the obvious problems have already been dealt with. So, in order to reflect reality, our first year target should be higher than the targets of later years. This way, we would be able to create short-term targets for each year that is relevant to the long-term target.

Targets are meant to be adjusted (if necessary).

Should we adjust our target values? Many people are concerned that if they allow target adjustment once, the target values might lose their reliability. This is true if we adjust our targets without decent reasons, or if organizations simply adjust their targets because they want to achieve a certain target value. In this case, you do not need a target at all, or you can just set a target once you know the result. In other words, shoot an arrow first, then put the bullseye where the arrow has landed. You just do not need a target; sound familiar? But if you do not allow any alterations at all, even if when the predefined targets are impossible to achieve, then your employees would have no motivation to work. Well, in such cases, you should allow target adjustment.

Now the question is in which cases should we allow target alteration? Targets should be adjusted when important incidents occur. First is when there is a strategic change. An adjustment in strategy has a direct effect on the target value of performance measures. For example, if we are making most of our sales through salespersons, we might set our target value to be an X number of sales per salesperson. However, if we add more distribution channels later on (e.g., modern trade channels), that means our sales strategy will change. At least, we need to take a look at our predefined target value for salespersons to see whether it is still valid or not.

Next is when there is a change in customer trends. Customer preferences are ever-changing. Sometimes, change happens very fast, but sometimes only gradually. For example, in the past, we used cameras to take photos, but now cameras are replaced with smartphones. Hence, we have to keep our target values (especially long-term) in check as trends change, to see if they need any adjustments.

The third incident is when there is an important event that greatly affects the current situation, such as 9/11, the tsunami in Japan, or wars. These things will affect our sales and other performance measures. We must review our targets to see whether or not they are still valid in such cases. Furthermore, if there is a request to adjust target values, we have to consider why we need the adjustment, because if we alter our targets without any proper reasons, in the end, those target values would lose their meaning,

There should be many levels of target values.

Let's talk about the risks of having "All or Nothing" one-level target values. Assume that I set a target of 1 million dollars for my salespersons, which will be rewarded with a three-month bonus plus a trip to Europe. However, if they cannot achieve it, they will get nothing at all. Is this target exciting and attractive? Well, if today is the first of January, then maybe yes, I would be able to motivate almost all of the employees, because everyone wants a three-month bonus and a trip to Europe. But what if some salespersons have already achieved one million dollars in sales by June, by the first half of the year? What would happen to their motivation to work? Of course, their motivation would decrease, because they have already achieved the target. There is no need for them to generate more sales, because they've already gotten all of the rewards. If you think about it, these employees who have lost their motivation are likely to be the company's top salespersons; otherwise they would not be able to achieve the target within the first half of the year. As time passes – July, August, September... – we would lose these salespersons.

Let's say it's October now. How many salespersons do you think would still be selling this company's products? Should be less than the beginning of the year. No, that is not enough... What? There is more? There will be another group of salespersons who haven't reached the goal but also have lost their motivation. These people are the ones who are way behind the target value. For example, by October, they only manage to generate 300,000 dollars in sales. They know that if they can only make 300,000 dollar sales in 10 months, they would not be able to achieve one million within three months. These people would give up, and the company will end up with very few salespersons by the end of the year. The rest of them are all on vacation.

See how having a one-level target value could be risky? And if that is so, how can we fix this problem? Let's see what could happen if we have a multi-level target value. Will it deal with the problem? And how? Using the same example, instead of setting the target value to be "All or Nothing," let's have a go with three levels. For example, if they can achieve 800,000 dollars in sales, they will receive a one-month bonus; one million dollars gets them a three-month bonus; and 1.5 million dollars gets them a five-month bonus plus a trip to Europe. This way, if our top salespersons have already achieved the one million dollars in sales within the first six months, they will not stop making more sales because there is a higher target waiting for them. Or if it is reaching the end of the year and some salespersons have only managed to generate 700,000 dollars in sales, they would not stop, because despite not being able to get the out-of-reach biggest reward, there are still other smaller rewards waiting for them.

Multi-level target values motivate more effectively than the one-level target values. But the thing is, achieving the highest level of target value decreases motivation. That is correct, and that is why we have to set the highest level to be challenging but achievable. This will help motivate everyone.

8 techniques for setting target values for performance measures

This is a checklist for those who are about to define target values for their performance measures:

1) Target values can be adjusted if there is a change in strategy, customer trends, and circumstances that affect performance measures.
2) Multi-level target values can motivate employees better than one-level target values.
3) The highest level of target values should be challenging but achievable.
4) Target value and rewards should be linked; the harder the target, the more attractive the reward.
5) Employees should be involved in setting target values, because they are the ones who will achieve it. If they do not feel like they own the target value, it would be hard to keep them motivated.
6) Past target values could be useful in setting new target values.

7) If there is no past data (maybe it is a new product), then customer and expert opinions could be a good source of reference in setting a new target value.
8) If competitor or industry average value is available, it could be used as a reference in setting a new target value.

Try adopting these techniques, and they might prove to be very useful.

Garbage in, garbage out

After we have a target, it is time for data collection. Have you ever heard of "Garbage In, Garbage Out?" Its meaning is very straightforward: *bad input = bad output*. It implies that if you have incorrect input, even advanced analysis and complex mathematics will not help make anything better, because the result will still be useless. Same goes for performance measurement. If we have carefully selected the best performance measures, but then we input incorrect data, the results will be incorrect. It will not matter at all how excellent our analysis is.

Therefore, information accuracy is one of the most significant factors in the performance measurement process. First things first. We need to ensure that the data is correct. Be careful when you ask your employees to punch in the data, so you do not end up getting a blank sheet of paper. This can mean two things: (1) Such data does not exist, and (2) The data exists but the employees refuse to input. Most of the time, number 2 is the case. But how can we encourage employees to punch in the correct data?

Let me tell you a story. In order to measure the percentage of defect, production employees have to fill in the number of defects, because they are the ones who produce defects and know best about it. However, it turns out that by the end of the day, the company only receives blank papers. There are two possible cases: (1) There is no defect today, or (2) There are defects like every other day, but the employees did not fill in the forms. I would suggest that number 2 is most likely the case, not number 1. If you do not believe me, then wait for a couple of more days. If number 1 is the case, there should be some defects on the next day because it is very unlikely that there will be no defects at all. If this were the case, then there would be no point for us to create the performance measure in the first place.

Firstly, we need to learn why the employees did not fill in the form. Maybe they simply do not understand it, or maybe they just do not see the importance of doing it. Actually, most of the time, it is because of fear. When employees need to provide information, especially a negative one like defects, they would naturally be afraid that once management receives the data, it might be used against them. For example, the management might reprimand them, reduce their salary, or even fire them. When employees are afraid, they will not provide true data. This is very important, because if we receive incorrect data, the performance measure would be useless, no matter how well it is designed. What we should do is to take away their fear, especially when what they fear is not even real. We have to inform the employees that the number of defects is not being collected to serve as a punishment. We do not collect the data to fire the employees, but rather to stop defect problems. We have to make them understand that performance measurement system is the tool that will help management eliminate problems, not employees.

Data are valuable, do not throw them away.

Have you ever noticed that data collection is not an easy task? Some people do not want to provide any information, because they are afraid that the information might come back to hurt them. Some people want to cooperate, but they do not understand what kind of data is needed. We can say that it takes "blood and tears" for some organizations to retrieve all the data they need.

Now let's assume that we have successfully retrieved all the data. The next question is, what should we do with it? This is also a vital step. The data that we have acquired must be arranged and be accessible, because these data have to go through data processing to be converted into various performance measure values, which would then be used to create reports. Is data collection software a must-have? The answer is that it depends on how complex your organization is. If it is highly complex and is a large organization with a huge amount of data, then data collection and management software should make everything easier for you. But for SMEs with few data, MS Access or Excel should be more than enough. More importantly, it is likely that the data that is collected during the early stages might not be 100% complete. No matter how well you prepare, there will still be misunderstandings, incorrect input, etc. Do not panic. If something is wrong, then fix it. For example, you can add more explanation to the form. If we just let it be, it could be harmful as the creditability of the performance measurement system will go down with it. And once your employees think the system is erroneous, do not expect them to use the data from the system ever again.

Before getting your hands on data collection

When we plan to measure our organization's operations, the first thing that we need to consider is data collection. Many organizations start off by designing a form for data collection. But hang on... Did you know that most of the time, the process by which you ask your employees to fill in the data becomes a barrier in data collection? Sometimes it even results in employees objecting to the idea of performance measurement.

Why is that so? Because sometimes the form that we use is the same as many other forms, so it turns out that the employees end up having to fill in the same data over and over again. So I recommend that you take a look and see if the data you need is already stored in your database or not. In other words, talk to your IT department first. If your organization is using an ERP (Enterprise Resource Planning) system, it is likely that you already have the data in your database, but it is collected for other purposes. If this is the case, then cool! You simply need to retrieve the data and analyze it to receive the performance measurement result that you are looking for. However, do not expect to have every single data in your database. That would be too much to expect. Most qualitative performance measures (measurement of feelings and emotions) are not stored, which brings us to yet another important point. If you do not have the data, do not abandon the performance measure. The reason why we come up with a performance measure is not because we already have data on hand, but because that performance measure is important. If you do not have the data, then you need to collect it. You can conduct a survey, an interview, or anything. As long as it is necessary, you must do it.

What should we do if data is not available?

Sometimes you might find yourself in a situation where you have already built a performance measure, just to realize later on that you cannot collect the data. What does "cannot collect the data" mean? You might find out that some types of data require more investment than your budget allows, or you might have the budget for it, but the value of the data itself is not worth the investment. So what should we do? Many people would just give up because they cannot collect the data. But hold on, do not give up so easily. If you do not have the data or lack the access, you can try using "surrogate performance measures." Surrogate performance measures might not be as effective as the normal performance measures, but it is better than nothing, right?

Let me give you an example. Assume that we want to design a customer satisfaction performance measure by conducting a survey to find the average satisfaction score. However, we find that each survey will cost quite a lot of money, and we cannot afford it. So, we should consider a way to measure other kinds of satisfaction that could substitute for the customer satisfaction score. We might find other performance measures like the repeated purchase rate, which may be data we already have. It should be able to reflect customer satisfaction more or less. This kind of performance measure is what we call "surrogate performance measure."

Oh, and one more thing, do not forget external data. Sometimes when we say we could not collect the data or that data collection requires high investment, these data might already be collected by external organizations, such as research institutions, ministries, and other public institutions. Last but not least, the phrase "unavailable data" is just another obstacle that we have to overcome.

Source of data

Now let's get to data collection. From where should we retrieve the data? Normally, there are four main sources:

1. Electronically stored data

These data may be stored for other purposes - financial data, for instance, are stored to be used in creating financial reports. Coming across these data is like finding lost treasure because we do not have to invest anything at all. We only need to retrieve the data, and can utilize it right away.

2. Data stored on paper

These data may be stored for other purposes as well. However, they might not have been uploaded to a digital database. For example, we might have the number of defects stored in monthly production reports. When we want to use these data for our defect performance measure, we can retrieve them from monthly reports without having to collect new data.

3. Data that need to be additionally retrieved from a digital platform

If our existing database does not have the data we want, then we have to collect additional data. My suggestion is, if possible, you should convert the data into digital format all at once, so that you can skip the punching in process during which mistakes often arise. An example of this would be using an employee card scanning system to collect data on absenteeism.

4. Data that need to be additionally retrieved from documents

This is the last source of information. If the first three sources are not available, collecting data from documents can be your last option. The reason why I want it to be the last option is because it is time consuming. Your employees might get so bored of it that they begin to object to the whole system. But if it really is necessary, then you have to do it – collecting employee satisfaction scores through a survey, for instance.

It seems like there are two main data collection systems. One is digital systems, which do not involve any paper documents, and the other is manual systems, which primarily rely on paper documents. Digital systems are easy and convenient, but require high investment, especially to build. Manual systems do not require much investment, but are time consuming and inconvenient. So organizations have to consider the pros and cons of each system.

How frequently should data be collected?

This is a very common question. Should we collect data daily, weekly, monthly, or annually for our performance measures? This question is about the "frequency" of data collection, which normally depends on two factors: the cost of data collection, and the changing rate of data.

Regarding the first factor, if each data collection incurs a high cost, then of course, we will not be able to collect data on a regular basis. Otherwise, our organization would go bankrupt. For example, if we have to invest one million dollars each time we collect customer satisfaction data by conducting a survey, we will not be able to collect the data daily and spend a million dollars every day. That would be too much to afford, or if we can afford it, it still would not be worth it.

Regarding the second factor, let's assume that the cost incurred is not that high. However, the changing rate of the data is quite low. In this case, we do not need to collect the data frequently. Let's say we use online questionnaires to retrieve employee satisfaction scores. No matter how many times we collect the data, the cost would not be that high. But still, we would not send out daily online questionnaires to our employees. Why not? Because employee satisfaction would not change much over the period of a day. Hence, collecting data that is unlikely to change frequently would incur unreasonable costs. Or if it does not incur a high cost, it would still attract unnecessary annoyance.

On the other hand, if the data is prone to change but we rarely collect it, we will not be able to see the trend. For example, you would not collect data on stock prices weekly, right? Because stock prices change every day, or even by the second. If you collect stock price data on a weekly basis, you will not be able to see the change in stock prices during the week. Well, it is like everyone says, "Too much or too little can both be bad." It is better to be "just about right." Now, many of you might still wonder how it's possible to know what it means to be "just about right." I have a suggestion to help you decide the frequency of data collection for each performance measure.

There is a study that states that we should collect data six times during the time of change of that performance measure to be able to see the trend clearly. For example, if we want to see the change in customer satisfaction over a period of six years, we should collect data annually. However, if we want to see the change in customer satisfaction over a three-year time period (because customers change frequently in this industry), then we should collect data once every six months. And if we participate in a fast-paced industry, we might want to analyze our customer satisfaction trend over a six-month time period. This means that we should collect data monthly. I believe this information should be beneficial for those who plan on collecting data. So, give it a try.

When should data be collected?

Once we have decided how frequently we are going to collect data, we also have to decide which day of the week, month, or year we are going to collect the data. We need to collect accurate data for our performance measure, which means that the time of data collection is also important. Mistakes usually occur when selecting the time of data collection. If we choose to collect data at inappropriate times, we might get incorrect data or data that does not reflect reality, which means the performance measure will be incorrect as well. And the rest is history.

Let me give you an example. Assume that we have already decided to collect customer satisfaction data from customers who use the service of a mall once a month. Then we ask our employees to distribute customer satisfaction questionnaires at 11 am on Monday. So, the employees go to the mall to distribute the questionnaire, and finish at noon. Now, it is time for us to process customer satisfaction data, analyze it, and make recommendations for future improvements. Have you noticed the potential mistake? If we only collect the data on a weekday morning, despite having enough numbers in our sample, we might only cover a specific group of customers. Plus, they might not even represent the majority of the mall's customers. If we collect data just so we can get it over with, our data would be no different from garbage, because we could barely use it or could not use it at all.

Who should be the data collector?

This is another common question, because, in many organizations, people try to evade the responsibility as it means that they have to work more than usual. Plus such task is very much hated by most people. However, the answer to this question is not that difficult. Firstly, if the data are already stored in the database, we would not need anyone to collect them. We simply have to ask the IT department to retrieve the data from the system, and then we can process the data right away. However, if such data does not exist and needs to be collected, the simple solution is to have the ones whose work is most relevant to that data collect it.

For example, if we have the number of defects designed as a performance measure, who should be the ones to collect this data? We have to go back and check to see which department is responsible for creating defects, which would be none other than the production department. Hence, in this case, the production department should be the one responsible for collecting the data. Having the responsibility of data collection does not mean that a particular department has to be responsible for the results alone. For example, if a salesperson is responsible for collecting daily sales data, it does not mean that he has to be held responsible for a decrease in sales. Sometimes the decrease in sales figures might be a result of poor production quality, bad advertisement, or many other things. In any case, someone should be responsible for data collection. Otherwise, you might end up with "performance measures with no data."

Cautions of data collection

It takes a lot of effort to acquire data, so we should take good care of the data collected. We should store it systematically. Even though we might have already processed and reported the data, we should still not throw them away, because we will never know when we have to utilize those data again for a different purpose, or we might even create new performance measures that require these past data.

The next caution of data collection is about data access restriction. Some data are sensitive to an organization's competitiveness such as cost of production. This is the kind of data that needs access restriction, because the higher the number of people involved, the higher the risk.

The last caution is computer viruses. I believe everyone has heard of or has experienced a computer virus before. Our data storage system should be secure. In addition, we should also back up the data in order to prevent data losses.

Chapter 10

Prepare a result report

In previous chapters, I discussed system design, target setting, and data collection. In this chapter, it is time for presenting the collected data. So let's take a look at important factors that we should pay attention to.

Do not fall at the last hurdle.

It is a shame that many organizations with good performance measures and data collection fail towards the end. "Failure" in this case means that no one utilizes the data. You can even say that the data report has somewhat become more of a homework that just needs to be handed in. After that, no one knows nor cares about what happens to it. It is a pity because reporting is one of the last processes. Designing a good performance measure and collecting accurate data require a lot of effort. But if it turns out that we fail at reporting, these processes would literally be worth nothing. Yes, it would be difficult to create a perfect report during early days. However, 75% is good enough for me. We can gradually adjust it toward perfection. Most of the time, bad reports are not a result of failed computer systems or miscalculations, but of poor understanding of performance measures or processes. So let's see how we can create an interesting report of performance measure results.

Prepare a "simple" report.

The first technique I would like to introduce for effective reports is to make them as simple as possible. Everyone likes the word "simple" – report creators like it, and so do users. Doing what everyone likes can lead to success. Think about it, if it takes us weeks to prepare a report, we would not want to do it, right? Plus, once the report is sent out to employees of each department, it would take them weeks to finish reading, and understand everything in the report. Do you think anyone would ever read such a report?

Therefore, the first rule of thumb is to make everything "simple." We must have a user-friendly report system. Let me give you an extreme example. If we can create a report within five minutes, that would be excellent. This is where a software or an IT system can be a great helper. It would take only a few minutes for users to understand the report and put it to good use right away. This is what is called "simplicity." Easy plus easy equals effortless. If this does not succeed, then I do not know what else can.

Prepare a "relevant" report.

Now let's take a look at another technique that could make a report more interesting. *Use a rifle, not a shotgun to hit the target.* What does that have anything to do with result reports? If you love American films, you would be familiar with how protagonists use a rifle gun. They would place the gun on their shoulder, which is why this kind of gun is highly accurate and hardly misses the target. The short gun is the opposite; it's hit or miss (but most of the time, miss). Preparing a report is like firing a gun. If you create a report like you shoot a rifle, your report will hit the target better. A report that is meant to be sent to the marketing department, should be designed specifically for the marketing department with relevant marketing data.

Likewise, a report for the production department should be designed specifically for the production department. This way, users will receive only relevant data. However, creating a report like you fire a short gun, trying to shoot everything in sight (e.g., you prepare one big report that contains the data of every department, then make multiple copies and distribute to everyone in the organization) is firing blind, expecting everyone to search for the relevant data on their own. I would say you are expecting too much. Most people would end up not reading anything in the report. This could be very heartbreaking for the people who work on preparing the report.

Think of the readers

When preparing a report, you have to ask yourself about who is going to be reading the report. It is a simple question that people rarely ask themselves. I have experienced this kind of complaint quite frequently: no one reads result reports anyway, what should we do? Before jumping right into adjusting the report, adding more colors and contents, the first question that we should answer is, "Who will be the readers of this report?" If we can answer this question, we would know what to do next.

If the report will be sent to the CEO, how much detail do you think you have to go into? If you have too much detail in the report, do you think the CEO will read it? What about the report for the CFO? What kind of contents do you think you should include? It has to be an executive overview instead of details, right? If the report is meant for head of the department, then you can add more details because he or she needs the details to solve problems. Or if you really do not know what that person wants, the easiest way is to ask him or her. Try this simple technique every time you are sitting in front of a screen, preparing a report – think of the readers.

Abolish the one-size-fits-all system

The key to creating a good result report system is to *decentralize. Do not stick to the principle of "One Size Fits All,"* because it is nearly impossible to have a form of report that is suitable for every department and every incident. Creating a standard form of report that does not consider what department the performance measure is from and the different data needs of departments, could make the report useless. Meaning, it would be hard to find relevant data, which would make the report uninteresting.

The public sector often uses this system, because it is easy to create, as they can simply design a single form for employees to fill in. Sometimes the employees can only fill a couple of answers in, but have to read through 100 questions to do so. Most of the time, they would fill in "N/A" or "0." To make matters worse, those data (that were not needed to be filled in) are created into tables and graphs. Therfore, the report only contains "N/A" values. No matter how useful this report could have been, it would still be dull because relevant data are all obscured by a pool of irrelevant data. So let's change how we do things. Let's prepare a report that contains relevant data for each particular department. This way, the report would be interesting. We can even add more details, explanations, and analysis, too. I believe that most people would be looking forward to read such a report and put it to good use.

Good news or bad news?

Have you ever noticed that sometimes reports contain good news, but from time to time they also contain points of failure? Let me give you an example. Let's assume that we have two possible ways to report a performance measurement result: 99% of our products passed quality standards, or 1% of our products failed quality standards. These two forms are called conformance reports (99% good quality products) and nonconformance reports (1% defects). Which one should we use? The answer is that it depends on the objective of the report. Conformance reports are commonly used to communicate with people outside the organization, and it portrays the good side, which would attract customers. Another advantage of this kind of report is that it sounds positive; it can motivate employees. Everyone loves good news. However, if reporting is for internal use to make further improvements, then nonconformance reports are used; 1% defects will be reported. This kind of report promotes continuous improvement, because if we say that we are 99% good, most people would perceive that the performance is already excellent, so there is no need to develop further. So, try to apply these two forms of reports in your organization.

Using indices in reports

An index is a value that is calculated by taking every performance measure into account. Let me give you an example. We might have many quality performance measures. However, to see an overall picture of our organization's quality, we need to calculate the index of all performance measures by adjusting the scores using the same scale. It is not necessary to give equal importance to each performance measure. We can assign a greater weight to important performance measures than the less important ones. Creating an index value can provide an overall direction on a particular matter. If you cannot picture this, try thinking of the stock market index. Stock market index was created to act as an indicator of overall market performance by including every stock price in the market calculations.

However, what you need to be aware of when using the index is that the more performance measure values included in the index, the lower the variation of the index would be. So, do not misinterpret the index value. When an index does not change, it does not always mean that every performance measure does not alter. When an index is stable, it might be caused by a great increase in certain performance measures, and a plummet in others. Same goes for the stock market indices. Stability of the stock market index does not imply that none of the stocks' performance changed. It is possible that half of the stock prices in the market have risen, while the other half have declined.

How to report "confidential" data

There is always a question on whether or not we have to report every single performance measure to workers. The answer is "we should," because otherwise they would not be able to improve. Another top question is, what if that performance measure is confidential. For example, should we report the performance measures that can put us at a disadvantage if acquired by our competitors, such as cost per unit?

Now this question is interesting because there is a risk of competitors acquiring our data. How can we know if one of our employees has a girlfriend who works at a competitor company? Or what if one of our employees switches to a competitor company? Having them sign a contract might still not be effective because we would never know when our employees are going to share our confidential data. It would be a little bit too much to ask them to swear on it. Yet, if we do not report results, performance measures would be of no use. For example, if we do not report the cost, then our employees would not know what the cost is, and consequently there would be no improvement. So, what can we do?

The answer is that we need to report it. However, it is not necessary to report the actual number. Am I saying that we should report wrong data? Not at all, but there is a way out. Instead of reporting the actual data, we can report "the rate of change" of that performance measure. For example, instead of reporting the cost per unit, we can report the rate of change in cost per unit to show the percentage of increase or decrease. Or we can utilize the score; meaning, instead of reporting the cost per unit, we can simply provide the score. The employees do not need to know how many dollars the score represents. Rather, they only need to know whether or not the cost has increased, which should be enough for them to work on improvements.

Another method is to report the index value. We could use a value from any year as a base value, and set it to 100 - I just made up this number, you would need to adapt it. If the cost increases by 10% next year, then the index would be 110. With this method, employees would have enough data for further improvement while we eliminate the risk of revealing confidential data to people outside the organization.

How many forms of reporting are there?

When it comes to reporting organizational performance measurement, there are many forms of reports we can utilize. Let's start with the most low-tech and probably the most common one: the paper-based report. This kind of report does not require high investment, all you need is a computer and a printer. However, the disadvantage of this method is that it is difficult to make changes in the future. Let's say the report's user needs the data to be in the form of a table rather than a graph. The user has to contact the report maker, and the user would never know if he would be able to get in touch with that person. Plus, we would never know when the report maker would finish creating the report. Then, there would be one revised version after another. The user might end up forgetting what data he has asked for in the meantime.

The next form, paperless reports, do not need to be printed out or bound. The most common format is a Word document or PDF, which would then be distributed through email. Users can read the report anywhere as long as they have a phone or laptop. There is no need to carry the report around, hence it is more convenient and cost (paper) saving. However, this form of report can still be difficult to edit.

Another from is a report created through a website. We only have to send a link to a particular website, together with the login credentials. This kind of report is getting more popular, because once a report is created, we can upload it to a website right away. We do not need to type report contents or send emails to each employee. More importantly, we can adjust the report automatically, by checking the login history to see which division or department the users are from. Once we know which department the users are from, we can choose to display only the data that are relevant to them. In addition, it would be easier to track download history and to see who never logs into the system. If the latter is the case, then there is problem.

Another form of performance measurement report – the online report - is a very good one, because it is both creator and user-friendly. With online reports, we can simply provide login credentials to users. The users can log on to the system to see relevant reports. A marketer can see marketing performance measures, while a financier might see financial performance measures. What makes it even better is that this form of report allows users to adjust the reports themselves through filters. Users can select which data they want displayed on the report, or create their own graphs. Users love this kind of report, because they can get anything they want in less than 10 seconds. The creator would be satisfied as well, since he or she does not have to create new graphs. It is a win-win situation. However, there is one small disadvantage to this kind of report. It requires investment in software. If you ask me whether or not it is expensive, I would say it depends on the benefits you receive from it. If your organization is big and has a lot of data, I would say the software is worth it.

And here comes the most advanced kind of performance measurement report. Like online reports, this form requires login credentials from users. When users log in, they see only the relevant reports, and can adjust the reports according to their needs. But what's amazing about this kind of report is that it offers real-time data – meaning that you can retrieve the data in real-time and they will always be updated. Let's assume that we are looking at sales revenues. Data collection would happen all the time at points of sale. We can see the graph move all the time, just like the stock market. How's that? Isn't it exciting? I have once joked with my students that it would be pretty exciting to have a real-time grade report. A real-time board would be set up at every desk. Whenever the students got bored and paid attention to their phone instead of listening to me, their grade would gradually reduce. Wouldn't that be great?

One company has adopted this system, and found something interesting. They measured the performance of their call center by allowing the customers who called in to assess them. Well, it does not sound that interesting when I put it this way. But here's the difference. An assessment system like this is randomized. They did not ask every customer to evaluate their performance, rather, they only asked some of them. Now a typical organization would gather this information and analyze it at the end of the week or month to assess employee performance. But not this company. This company calculated customer satisfaction right away, and displayed the result in real-time on their employees' computer screens, as they responded to customer questions. What's even more exciting is that this company used this performance measure to determine employee bonuses. Can you guess how the company did that? They finalized their evaluations by the end of every shift. After every shift, the employees would know whether or not they would receive a bonus for that day. Customer satisfaction performance measure was used as a criterion. If the employees could achieve the predefined goal, then every employee working during that shift would receive a bonus. However, if they could not achieve it, no one would get a bonus.

Oh, one more thing... The customer satisfaction score displayed on the employees' screens an average score that did not belong to anyone in particular. And that score was used as a bonus criterion. So, how is that? Isn't it exciting? However, in the end, this system failed, and the company had to discontinue it. Before we go any further, let's think about why this system might have failed? What could be the reasons behind it? Can you come up with any? If not, I'll give you a little more time...

Here's the answer. Many people might guess that this kind of system would stress out the employees. Well, that is part of the reason. If anyone gets measured while they are working, they would stress out. But the main cause of the failure is that the customers called to complain. But why is that? This system should benefit the customers because the employees would have to take good care of customers, right?

Here's what happened. Many customers called to complain that they had been experiencing something weird lately. For example, if they made a call during a certain time, they would get bad responses. Let's say if they called around 4 pm, the employees would talk to them impolitely, and did not serve them well. Sometimes they said that the service was absolutely terrible. But if they called during other times, the service would be good. They had tried calling several times, and they still experienced the same thing. What happened?

First, let's look back at the real-time measurement system. This system is good because it can tell the average satisfaction score right away. But there is a disadvantage to that... Once the employees know the customer satisfaction score in real-time, they know whether or not they will get a bonus for that day. So, when it is near the end of the shift - let's say the shift ends at 4 pm – each call center employee knows for certain whether they are receiving a bonus or not, because the score is displayed in real time. If the customer satisfaction score is far behind the goal, they would know that they would not be able to make up for the loss in the next 5 minutes. You can guess what would happen next... Employees do not have to work hard anymore, so it is unfortunate for the customers who call during that time. This kind of situation would happen when the customer satisfaction score is way above the goal near the end of the shift as well. The employees know for certain that they would get a bonus for today, so let's just sit back and relax. This is the reason why this system had failed. It is kind of unexpected, right?

Manual reports vs. electronic reports

So which one is better: paper-based reports, aka. manual systems, or digital systems that require software? In order to answer this question, we have to take a look at three factors:

1. The amount of investment you are willing to make

Manual systems barely need any investment at all except for a computer and a printer. However, in practice they can prove to be difficult to use. Let's say the user needs to adjust the graph or request additional information. This means that you would have to recreate the graph and table, print, and send out the revised report. If users rarely make extra requests, then it would not be very difficult. However, if there are a lot of requests, you might have to hire a team to deal with it, which means higher cost. If you use a digital system, of course, you would need to invest in software and system installations; however, it would make everything much easier in the long run, and users can work on the revisions themselves.

2. The size of your organization

When organizations are complex, digital systems could be of great help. However, when it comes to SMEs with small numbers of employees, manual systems should be more suitable; it is harder to make adjustments in larger organizations than in smaller ones.

3. The characteristics of the report

If the report is a standard one, meaning it has a definite template, then manual systems should be fine, because you know for certain that the form of the report will never change (very common among government reports). However, if you have to adjust the report according to the users' needs, then you would be better off with a digital system.

All in all, regardless of the report's form, the most important thing is that the readers have to be able to understand and utilize the report.

How to make reports user-friendly

I have five main suggestions that would help make people read reports:

1) People can digest no more than seven items at a time. Therefore, do not include more than seven kinds of data in a single graph or table.
2) People usually look at the data at the center of the page first. Hence, you should place important data in the center of the page.
3) Pictures are easier to understand than texts. Therefore, if possible, you should utilize pictures.
4) Use simple diagrams rather than pretty ones that look complicated.
5) You can adjust your report presentation to be more interesting by utilizing other forms of graphs, or using colors.

Try putting these five recommendations into action, and your report might become more interesting.

Graph lines are also important

The graphs that we usually see contain a line that shows a performance result. However, I want to introduce two more graph lines that will show performance measure results, which would make the graphs more useful.

The first line is called the baseline. This line tells you the performance result during early stages, before work process development took place. This line would be like the startline of a running race. The other line is the benchmark or target. This line is the finish line that we want to reach. Adding these two lines to your graph will help you see the direction of that particular work process outcome - whether or not you are on the right path. If the line starts from the baseline and is moving toward the benchmark, then you can sit back and relax. However, if this is not the case - for example, the performance is still around the baseline, or is turning away from both the baseline and benchmark - you have to fix that immediately.

Management cockpit

Nowadays, many companies have changed the layout of their meeting rooms. They do not just have air condition, TV, or new paint; these ordinary meeting rooms have become extraordinary. Instead of having cement walls or beautiful paintings, there are KPI graphs on walls. This kind of room is called the "management cockpit." As its name suggests, the cockpit is the room for the pilots to control an airplane. If you have visited a cockpit before, you would see that a cockpit has various gauges – altimeter, fuel gauge, direction radar, and other gauges that pilots have to use to fly safely to the destination. Why do pilots need these gauges? The simple answer is, because flying an airplane is very complicated. Even when we drive a car, we still need a dashboard.

However, I believe we would still manage to drive without a dashboard. On the other hand, flying an airplane without a dashboard would be very difficult. If you got on an airplane and do not see it in the cockpit, better leave the airplane immediately. Pilots are able to control airplanes thanks to these gauges, especially when flying at night or at high altitudes. Without these gauges, flying would be very hard. Imagine how much damage would be caused if the gauges did not work. Same goes for organizations. The more complex the organization is, the more necessary gauges are for the management to manage and lead the organization to success.

Chapter 11
Do not use it if it fails a test

We should be done with designing a performance measurement system after we have designed performance measures, collected data, and reported the results. But for certitude, we should test the system before launch. Testing would allow us to determine the cause of potential problems so that we can fix them before starting to use the system. Let's see what we need to check.

#1 Test the relevancy to strategy.

As I have mentioned earlier, a good performance measurement system reflects the organization's strategy. But how can we know whether our performance measurement system is aligned with the strategy or not? This is a very interesting question. You can simply put it on trial. If the predefined strategy gets translated into action, which results in a certain outcome, that means the system works. If not, then the system does not work. This answer is not a simple answer, but rather a convenient one. Well, it's like we build a car and when a person asks us, "Is this car safe?", and we simply reply, "Go on a test drive. If it does not explode, then it's safe." This is not a nice reply at all.

After we have finished designing an organizational performance measurement system, we should test it. The first test is to see *whether the system is aligned with the organization's strategy or not*. The best way to test is to take the system to the executive management team, and discuss with them. They are the ones who develop the strategy, hence they would know whether the performance measures match their strategy or not. Most of the time, designing a performance measurement system takes a long time, and there are many adjustments along the way. Or sometimes there are changes in the organization's strategy. Testing ensures that what we measure covers the key points in the strategy; no more, no less.

#2 Test the validity of the performance measure.

Having tested strategic relevance, the next step is to test the validity of performance measures. How can we know whether our performance measures give us the correct values or not? I think this is a very good question as well. You can try the following methods to check if your performance measures give the correct results or not.

1) Take a look at important business processes: production, customer management, etc.; and see if there is any performance measure that is controlling these procedures. If not, the number of existing performance measures is not enough.
2) Ask yourself how effectively the existing performance measures demonstrate the changes in those procedures. Assume a performance measure determines the % of defects – let's say if the number of defects increases, the value of this performance measure would rise immediately, which shows that the performance measure works. However, if your performance measures can only show whether there are defects or not, meaning that you would not be able to tell if the number of defects have increased, then that performance measure does not work, because it can only tell that "there are" defects.

3) Try checking the correctness of the existing performance measures by collecting data and calculating the results manually. Do not trust the IT system or software, before you get to compare the results with your manually calculated number first.
4) Try plugging in made-up numbers to test the system once again. For example, if you know that the % of defects is calculated by dividing number of defects by number of produced goods, then key in 10 pieces for defects and 100 pieces for produced goods. The accurate system should return 10%.
5) Try adjusting the numbers from step 4. For example, instead of typing in 10 pieces, try keying in 50 pieces (with 100 pieces of produced goods), and see whether the number changes from 10% to 50% or not. You can do this multiple times to validate.

Try adapting these five suggestions to your organization.

#3 Test data accuracy

Another significant component in creating organizational performance measurement systems is data accuracy. Before using the system, you have to ensure that your data is accurate. But how can you be sure of that? You have to test it first. The easiest way to test is to enter all data into the system, and examine the result of each performance measure. Strange results might indicate that there is something wrong with the data. Beware of performance measure results that show no data; most of the time, this is caused by a system error, not because there is no data to process.

#4 Test the correctness of reports.

How can we know that our performance measure reporting system is working? The simplest way to do this is to create a report, and take it to its users. This might take us some time in the case of paper reports for example, because we would have to send the report out, and wait for users to read it before we can ask for their opinions. Or if the reports are digital, we have to allow the users some time to familiarize themselves with the system, before asking them for feedback.

I recommend creating an open-ended simple questionnaire that allows users to express their opinions – what should be improved, for instance – so that we can use these recommendations to improve our report. It does not sound that difficult at all, right? If you already have this kind of report in place, have you ever asked the users for their opinions to see if they like the report or not? Do not forget – a report without readers is nothing but scrap paper.

#5 Test to see if the system will be put to use.

When we build a performance measurement system, we do not only expect precise performance measures, usable data, and an interesting report of results; we also hope that the system will be used in a beneficial manner. Hence, one of the things we should test, is whether the users have utilized the performance measure system or not. But how can we test that? A simple answer to this question is to let the users test the system. If it is a digital one, then give them usernames and passwords. After a week, you can ask them if they got to use the system. Or if it is a manual system, ask them how they utilize the data in their job. If we find out that they get to use the data, then we can rest easy. But if not, we might need to find "the reasons why," otherwise the system would become useless.

#6 Test to see if the system has any other uses.

This is the last topic about testing. Do not stop asking questions, even if you have received positive user feedback. Do they have any other suggestions? Or even if the users say the system is useless – do not give up, because what's useless to one person might be useful to another. Sometimes a system designer cannot see how the system can be adapted to other kinds of usage. So try asking this question, and you might find that the system that you have is more useful than you thought.

Three questions that need to be answered after testing

Once we finish testing, we might receive suggestions, criticisms, or even complaints on why we did not do this and that. I think this is very normal. It is better than not having anyone paying any attention at all. In fact, if you look on the bright side, those criticisms actually stem from good will. If one does not care, why would he/she give any suggestions at all, right? But what should we do? Should we follow what they said, or stand by what we think is right? If we choose to follow what they said, how much should we compromise? If we stand by what we think is right, will it seem like we listen to nobody?

The simple answer to this is that we should take those suggestions into consideration. If the answers to the following three questions are "yes," then you should follow the suggestions. However, if one of the answers is "no," then you should not follow the suggestions, and go back and explain your reasons to the users as to why you did not follow their suggestions. The three questions are:

1) Does the suggestion have a solid rationale?
2) Is the suggestion practically possible?
3) Do we have enough resources, and is it worth the change?

The first question is "Does the suggestion have solid a rationale?" Well, if you ask this question, everyone who has given the suggestion would say, "Of course," right? But the point of this question is to understand whether or not there are "enough" reasons to change the current performance measurement system or not. For example, if there is a suggestion that you should not use a certain performance measure simply because you have never used it before, it should not stop you from using it.

The second question: "Is the suggestion practically possible?" Of course, many people would say that it is possible. But sometimes they think their suggestions are possible due to a lack of information. A suggestion on comparing our cost with the competitor's sounds reasonable. However, it is nearly impossible for us to know the competitor's cost, so there is still a problem with this suggestion.

The last question: "Do we have enough resources and is it worth the change?" Sometimes suggestions are rational and are possible, but there is a lack in budget or other resources. For example, conducting a survey on customer satisfaction instead of just measuring the repurchase rate alone sounds like a rational and possible suggestion; however, there is a budget constraint. Hence, we could not conduct the survey.

If you find yourself stuck on any of the three questions, please explain to the one who gave suggestions that you have already carefully considered the suggestion, so that he or she could understand the reasons of rejection. However, if your answers are all "yes," meaning that the suggestion is rational, possible, is good value for money, and demands an appropriate amount of resources, then you should make the adjustment. Do not let your ego seize the development of your performance measurement system. Do not forget, Ego = 1/Knowledge.

Chapter 12
Implement a performance measurement system

Having created a performance measurement system, it is now time to implement it. So let's see what the key points of this process are.

Designing is hard, but using is harder.

Anyone who has been involved with organizational performance measurement should agree with the statement above. A performance measurement system that has not been put to use is nothing but a stack of blank papers. The first question is, how will the system be put to use? In general, there are two methods to choose from: apply to the whole organization at the same time, or apply to one division after another. If your organization is small, the first choice should be fine. However, if your organization is large, I would recommend starting with one division first, aka. a pilot program. An advantage of launching a pilot program is that you can learn about the system first, because you have no experience in it. You can limit the damage it could cause, should the system have any errors. You can utilize what you have learned from the pilot program to improve the system, and apply the revised version to other divisions of the organization.

Another benefit is that if you do not have a sufficient amount of human resources, a pilot program would allow you to delegate your human resources and time efficiently in order to deal with potential problems. Imagine starting to apply the system to the whole organization at once. Employees would ask so many questions that we might not be able to answer or deal with them on time, which might then lead to failure. Lastly, focusing on only one division could increase the success rate. And once the system has proven to be successful, it can be set as an example for other divisions, which would make organization-wide system adoption easier.

Where should we start implementing the system?

Having discussed pilot programs for performance measurement systems, let's now talk about where we should start putting the system to use. This is another interesting question. Normally, we would start where problems occur the most. Why is that? Starting where the problems occur most often, would make it easier to identify problems and see the results clearly, after the problems have been dealt with. Similar to building a software to remove computer viruses. If we start off by scanning computers that have no viruses, the results would show that there is no virus. However, users would doubt whether there really is no virus or the software simply does not work. But if we scan a computer with many viruses, the software would be able to detect the viruses so that we can deal with them. Wouldn't that look more impressive?

Same goes for performance measurement. We should identify the department with most problems first, in order for our performance measurement system to detect problems and recommend solutions. Once the problems have been solved, other departments would be willing to try out the system. Another thing is that if we start with a department with many problems, there is more for us to gain than to lose. If there are already many problems, solving them should make things better – or simply put, it would be difficult for us to make things any worse. However, starting with an excellent department would be more risky, because we would have to make what's already excellent better - that can be very difficult. And if things turn out good, employees might still doubt whether the performance measurement system really helped make things better or not, because the department was already great before the system.

The last question is, which department has the most problems? Sometimes you can answer this question easily by experience. However, if you do not know the answer, you would have to take a look at the work processes. The departments with many problems are usually the ones in the latter part of processes. It does not necessarily mean that those departments are the ones who create problems – sometimes the problems are accumulated from previous processes. In the next section, I'll show you what kinds of concerns you have to address before putting a performance measurement system to use.

Point of concern #1: Why should we have a performance measurement system?

"Why should we have a performance measurement system?" – this question frequently arises when we implement a performance measurement system in an organization. There are two answers to this question:

1) Performance measurement tells you the current status of your organization, whether it is good or bad.
2) Once you know the result, you would know which area you need to improve.

You lose almost nothing by measuring performance. Although some people might say that performance measurement is a waste of time, money, and labor, considering what you could gain from it, most would agree that it is worth it. Organizational performance measurement is like getting a health checkup. We have to pay money to get our health checked, but in return, we get to know how we should adjust our daily routine. I think that is really worth the money.

Point of concern #2: How can we use a performance measurement system?

If an organization's employees have no previous experience with a performance measurement system but one day their organization makes an announcement, "We are going to use KPI from now on," I believe many employees would be confused and nervous. They would be concerned about how the KPI is going to affect them. In fact, organizational KPI application is not as frightening as you might think. Instead, what you should be more worried about is using it the wrong way. Utilizing a performance measurement system would affect employees in the following procedures:

1) Employees play a part in the necessary data collection.
2) Collected data are transformed into performance measures.
3) The results will be analyzed to identify problems or opportunities in order to improve work processes.
4) Employees develop their work processes, and look forward to seeing the future results of performance measures.

And that actually covers everything. If you did great on everything, your organization would only flourish. And when your organization flourishes, your employees would receive rewards, such as bonuses or salary raises. A win-win situation.

Point of concern #3: Would we get punished if a performance measurement system is in place?

Before answering this question, I would like to ask you if you've ever gotten your health checked before. Why did you get your health checked? Didn't you have to pay for it? Many would simply answer, they did it to know their health condition, so it is worth the money. If they know that they are healthy, they would feel at ease and realize that they are living their lives correctly. And no one would complain, "What a pity. I want to be sick because I've already paid for the checkup." Also, if there is something wrong with your health, then you would be able to deal with it right away. For example, if you know that you have high cholesterol (LDL), you could get on with a healthy diet and exercise to recover your health, right? But what does this have to do with organizational performance measurement?

I've always compared organizational performance measurement to health checkups. We measure to improve, **not to harm people in our organization.** I always emphasize this point. We have to make everyone understand that performance measurement is a tool to help management and employees work together to solve problems. It is not a tool for management to fire employees - this mindset is very important. If employees' mindsets suggest otherwise, then performance measurement will fail.

Point of concern #4: Why does it have to be me?

"Why do you have to measure 'my' work results?" "Don't you trust me anymore?" These questions are frequently asked when a performance measurement system is about to be applied in the organization. First things first. Have you noticed the word "me" in the question? Once there is "me," there is "them," right? Questions stemming from this kind of a mindset marks the beginning of a conflict. Hence, it is vital to make everyone understand the rationale before starting to use a performance measurement system. There should be no "me" or "them." Performance measurement measures the "organization." The main objective is to utilize the results for organizational development, not to point fingers at and punish someone. Therefore, this whole thing is not about trust at all. Rather, performance measurement will point out problems for everyone to see and fix.

Point of concern #5: Why do we have to measure when everything is already good as is?

"Our organization has been established for 10 years. We didn't need any performance measurement. We didn't have any hardship. The profit is good. Why do we have to measure performance now?" This is probably another question that employees might ask themselves, or even say it aloud once they know there will be performance measurement, because they do not feel comfortable with it. In fact, I think this is a very good question, because it is an opportunity to register a new mindset in your organization. This is how I would like to answer this question. The fact that your organization has survived, and remained profitable for 10 years without performance measurement is a good thing. However, not facing any hardship without performance measurement for 10 years does not necessarily mean that you can survive another 10 years without hardship, right?

Let's say we meet a 40-year old person who has been recommended to get his health checked, and he says, "I've already lived for 40 years without any health checkups, and I'm doing just fine. Why do I need a health checkup now? Why do I have to waste my money?" Not having had any health checkups for 40 years, and not having any illnesses does not guarantee that the person will be able to live another 40 years in good health, right? This is the exact same thing – if we never check our organization's health through performance measurement yet our organization remains profitable, it does not guarantee the organization's survival in the future. In contrast, it could be very risky not to measure, since we might have accumulated many problems. Despite the fact that we are still profitable, it might mean that the problems are still hidden, the economy is good, the problems are tolerable, or customers are still fine with waiting for late delivery to arrive. However, when the economy turns sour, our organization might be the first to fall. If we were to start using performance measurement at that time, it would be too late. It is like giving a gravely ill person a health checkup – it is just too late.

Sometimes we might have heard, "We manage to generate profit without performance measurement. Why do we have to change now?" The above statement sounds reasonable – if something is already good, why change it? But the important question is, how do you know that "it's already good"? If you do not measure, then you have to use your own judgment. If you use your own judgment, you are putting your organization in a risky position. Some people might say, "Just look at the annual profit over the years! How can you say it's not good? Yes, making profit is good, but the profit could be a by-product of positive external factors, such as a good economy or an expanding market that allows you to sell anything. It could turn out that these good things are hiding problems. We might have too much inventory, frequently broken machines, or lazy employees, but they might not have affected our organization so far because we might have been able to generate profit regardless.

These problems are like rocks under the water. If the water level is high, boats would get through very easily. However, if the water level is low, the rocks would surface, making it difficult for boats to float. Same goes for organizations. Without performance measurement, we would not know if there is a problem or not. If we wait until the positive external factors disappear – poor economy and shrinking market – before identifying the source of the accumulated problems, it might be too late. Even if you might believe that your kind of industry would never go bad, still, with performance measurement, you might be able to generate a much higher profit than without performance measurement, because performance measurement tells you what the problems are, so that you can deal with them. Wouldn't it be better if you could get rid of the rocks under the water before they could create any damage to the organization? Performance measurement never harms anyone - only poor performance measurements do.

Point of concern #6: Why do they have to start with our department? Will we get to know the result?

There are two other common questions. "Why do they have to start with our department?" Most of the time, this question arises when we choose a certain department for a pilot program. The employees are curious as to why it has to be them. This question can be answered easily. You have to explain to your employees that, in the end, performance measurement would be applied to the whole organization, but you choose to start with this department first, because you can see the success opportunity in this department and this department can be a leading example for other departments in the organization.

The other frequently asked question is, "Will we get to know the results of the performance measures?" It is even easier to answer this question – "Of course." If the people who get measured do not get to know the results, then why are we measuring at all? After all, the people who can improve the work processes are these same people. If these people do not know the results, then performance measurement will not create any benefits.

When should we start using it?

Once the system is ready, there will be a question like "Eh, when should we officially start using it?" Monday, Tuesday, Wednesday, Thursday, Friday, or maybe Saturday or Sunday? I would like to skip the part about the auspicious day to launch a system in this book. In fact, prior to saying which day we should start using the system, we should define what "start using" really means first. When we apply a performance measurement system in an organization, in general, we would refer to the "first day of data collection." In fact, you can start on any day. But if possible, it should match the cycle of that particular performance measure's result report – that would be ideal.

Let me give you an example. If a defect performance measure is collected monthly, then the first day of data collection should be the first day of the month. Once we reach the end of the month, we would get a report for the whole month. However, if we start on the 15th, we would only get results for half of the month. In addition, we would have to spend more time to explain why we only have a half-month report for this month, and that for next month it is going to be a full-month report. This would add to the confusion, especially during the early days of launching a new system. We would make things more difficult than they have to be. Another thing we should do is to communicate the launch date of the system. If most of the employees do not know anything about the system, it would only make things more complicated.

Training, training, training

Training should be available during the early stages of performance measurement implementation. You cannot simply arrange a training session just to get it over with, as it requires good preparation. The level of success in training depends on the level of effort in preparation. The more you prepare, the more likely the training is to yield the best result. In the early stages of performance measurement system adoption, there will be complications and questions. The best way to prevent further confusion is to train people. Training sessions can be arranged using different methods – lectures and system trials, for instance. Normally, the training instructor is on the system design team, because he or she knows the system the best. However, if the system designer does not have good presentation or teaching skills, I would like to recommend that you hire someone with good basic teaching skills, and inform him or her with the details of the system. Also, the instructor should be a specialist in this field. These would ensure the success of the performance measurement system training.

Why is it so complicated? Why are there so many questions?

During the early days of performance measurement system application, there will be questions and complaints about why the system is complicated and why they have a lot of questions. I always reply, "It's good that they have questions," because if no one asks questions and keeps quiet, it is usually a bad sign showing that no one cares about the system. Therefore, it is good to receive many questions, because it means that people are actually paying attention. Furthermore, these questions will help you identify which areas users are still unclear about, so that you can clarify it for them. If you want users to have questions, you have to provide contact channels for them. My suggestion is to provide as many contact channels as possible - phone, email, chat, or other channels - because the more channels available, the more convenient it is for employees to ask questions.

If there is a question, there is an answer. During the early stages, it might be necessary to hold a daily meeting for the team. For example, you can have a discussion session for asking and answering questions. Or if there are any suggestions, the team could decide together whether to adjust the measurement or not. Although you might not end up following the suggestions in the end, you still have to reply to the people who asked the questions or gave suggestions to let them know the reasons behind your decision. Or if you do follow the suggestions, in addition to responding to them, you have to let every user know that there will be a change. This method should guarantee success than any other method available.

How can we know if the system succeeds or not?

How can we know if our performance measurement system "succeeds"? We would know if our employees utilize the performance measurement results in their jobs. In order for that to happen, performance measurement results have to reflect the true performance outcome. We have to invest money and labor for all these to come true. There should be a training session to establish mutual understanding, answer questions, or even fix problems. The more we do, the more we gain; the less we do, the less we gain. Well, what if it does not succeed? We have to take a step back and reevaluate everything to see what's wrong. Typical system failures are due to the following four reasons:

1) Management never really pays attention to the system.

   This is one of the top reasons, and is the hardest one to solve. Many managers use performance measurement only because other companies are using it. They lose interest in performance measurement after a while, and start seeking other kinds of tools. No system would survive with a mindset like this.

2) Employees do not understand the information that they receive.

   Many organizations have good and beneficial performance measures. However, due to ineffective communication, employees cannot comprehend the performance measures.

What are they reflecting? For what can employees use them? In the end, employees do not utilize the data, which is a shame.

3) Employees receive irrelevant data.

   Sometimes they understand the result of performance measures, but they do not use it because it is not relevant to their jobs. You have to beware of this. Do not send them the data just to get it over with – you have to ensure that the data is relevant to their jobs.

4) Employees receive incorrect data.

   If the performance measure is good and relevant, but the data is always incorrect, how can employees utilize it?

These are the four common problems. If you find out that your employees do not use the performance measurement system, you should go back and take a look at the reasons why, so that you can fix the problems accordingly.

Signs of acceptance

After implementation, would you like to know how you can tell if the system is widely accepted or not? The following incidents demonstrate that your employees have already adopted the performance measurement system into their jobs:

1) How-to questions about the performance measurement system have declined.

2) Criticisms regarding the performance measurement have ceased.
3) Employees have requested adjustments to the report format, such as changing the graph format or asking for additional data.
4) When the report is late, users ask when they will receive it.

Getting everyone to utilize the performance measurement system in their jobs does not necessarily mean that this system will always be perfect. As a person who is responsible for organizational performance measurement, you always have to ask yourself, "Is the data users receive relevant to their jobs?" and "Is this system still user-friendly?" These questions should allow you to adjust the system to align with the tasks, and make it sustainably beneficial.

Chapter 13
Put the data from performance measure to good use

There are many organizations that design good performance measurement systems that is very well-received by their employees. However, it is a shame that these organizations do not receive much benefit from the performance measurement system. In fact, it is not completely useless, because they have analyzed why certain performance measures have increased, while others decreased. Still, the benefits that they receive is less than what they should be. This is like buying a convertible car but only driving it to the market and back. That's a shame. Now let's see what benefits you can receive from analyzing and evaluating a performance measurement system.

Do not rush to analyzing the result.

When we receive the data from a performance measure, the first thing we normally do is to check if the value has increased or decreased, and why. Well, that does sound like the thing we should do, right? No! Because that is jumping to the explanation part, you have to consider the fact that changes in the value of performance measure are common. Think about the probability, it is more likely that the value changes than remain static (because there is only one possibility of the value being stable.)

Do you want to bet with me on whether the stock market index value will be different on Monday and Friday of this coming week? You probably wouldn't bet at all. Because everyone knows that it is nearly impossible for any stock market index value to remain stable throughout the week. What I am trying to say is that the value of a performance measure either increases or decreases. There is a possibility that it might remain stable, but that could hardly ever happen. What does this have to do with anything? Before you start analyzing why the performance measure has changed, you should consider the following characteristics:

1) The change is usual. There is nothing special.

For example, a daily increase or decrease of 5 points in the value of the stock market index is nothing special, because it would be difficult for the stock market index value to be totally stable. If there is such a change, do not waste your time explaining why. Sometimes I notice that some analysts trying to explain every time there is a change in the stock market index value. For example, they would say that the stock market index has decreased by 5 points because of poor economic conditions. And the next day, when the stock market index increases by 5 points, they just say that it indicates a change in the direction of the economy - there are only good news. Well, does the economy change every day?

2) There is a change due to a special incident.

This change is abnormal. For example, the stock market index has increased or decreased by more than 20%. This is this kind of change that you should take the time to identify the source of, because you normally do not observe the stock market values increase or decrease by 20% every day.

Try following this suggestion when you have to analyze your organizational performance measures, and you will be able to manage time and labor efficiently by choosing to analyze only important matters.

Do not panic because of what you just saw.

Oh my god, our sales declined 30% this quarter! Yes, this might be bad if... There's an "if"? The sales have declined by 30%, how can it be good? Of course, it can. Performance measures will show you things of concern if they are "abnormal." Let's say sales had always increased by 10% every quarter, but this quarter, sales declined by 30%. Something must have happened. As the person to analyze the performance measure, you have to identify the cause. What if it is normal? For example, you are selling a New Year's card, and your sales at the beginning of the year have dropped dramatically when compared to the end of last year. Then you do not have to worry about it, even if the sales dropped by 30%. If you take a look at past data, and compare them to the same quarter of previous year, you would see that it is normal.

Therefore, before you jump right into analyzing the results, I want you to see if the change is "abnormal" or not. If it is "abnormal," then start analyzing in detail. If it is normal, then do not panic, and do not spend time in analyzing the result - it would be a waste of time.

Correlation is also important.

The following conversation happens in a department that works in analyzing organizational performance.

Employee 1: "We're doing good this quarter. Customer satisfaction has improved."

Employee 2: "Yes, yes. But actually other performance measures have improved as well."

Employee 1: "True. Employee satisfaction has also improved."

Once this conversation is over, the two employees go back to work. One of them starts to write an analysis on the increase in customer satisfaction, while the other writes about the improvement in employee satisfaction. In fact, there is nothing wrong with that. Each person is doing their job. But what's missing is the correlation between the two performance measures if we analyze them separately.

We do not need to use any advanced statistics. We only have to plot the customer satisfaction score on the same graph as the employee satisfaction score. Sometimes, we will get to see a certain pattern. For example, every time employee satisfaction increases, customer satisfaction increases as well, or vice versa. Once you see the pattern, performance measure analysis would be more useful. So instead of analyzing the two performance measures separately, try analyzing them together – it could change the way you run your business.

Analyze from many angles.

The following event might have happened at your office.

Boss: "Eh, why do we get so many complaints from customers? Go take a look at which product model customers complain about the most."

Subordinate: "Sure thing, boss."

The subordinate comes back after 10 minutes.

Subordinate: "Model 323."

Boss: "We should arrange a meeting tomorrow to brainstorm on how we can improve this model."

Subordinate: "Great."

After that, everyone goes back to their desks to work. A week later, a meeting is held, and model 323 has been improved. Have you noticed anything strange? If you only skim through it, everything seems to be normal. But if you look into it in detail, the solution was already there when the boss asked his first question.

"Go take a look at '*which product model*' customers complain about the most."

The question contains an important assumption: the product model is the cause of the complaints. Of course, there will always be a product with the highest number of complaints. So, the company will end up improving that product model.

I used this example to illustrate that once you have received a performance measurement result, the first thing you should do is to consider many angles. You should not ask only which product model has been complained about the most. You should try to think of other possible causes as well – which factory produces most of the product with highest number of complaints, or which dealer has sold most of the product with highest number of complaints? Analyzing performance measurement results from various angles could change your perspective on problems. In the end, you will be able to fix the problem at its root cause.

Do not believe in the correlation right away.

In one of the previous examples, I suggested that you plot two performance measures on a single graph to see the correlation. In this section, I want to show you that the correlation might not always be the causation. Why is that? A correlation between performance measure A and performance measure B could be due to various reasons.

Firstly, the correlation could be purely coincidental, especially if you did not collect enough samples. For example, if you plot the height of 2-3 employees and their salaries, you might find out that the taller the employee, the higher their salary, which is very unlikely. This kind of situation happens from time to time; they plot so many graphs that they come across a strange correlation. For example, they found a correlation between the budget of science, space, and technology in the USA, and the rate of suicide by hanging or suffocation. There was a correlation between the number of deaths from drowning in a pool and the number of movies Nicholas Cage has starred in. There are so many other examples. But these should be enough to prove that correlations do not necessarily imply causal relationships.

Secondly, there is another important factor to consider in analyzing correlations. However, we have not yet included that factor in our analysis. Let me give you an example. Have you ever noticed that whenever a police is out directing traffic, there will always be a traffic jam? There is even a belief that "police creates the traffic jam." I believe many people have complained about something like this before, but do not jump to conclusions. Have you ever noticed that on Sunday morning, when we rarely get to see the police, there is no traffic? Well, then of course, it must be "the police that cause the traffic jam."

If someone counts the number of police seen on the road, and the time it takes to commute to one's destination, and plots a graph, we might get to see a positive correlation between the two – the more police you see, the worse the traffic. Now, can we draw the conclusion that the police cause traffic jams? Not yet. According to the findings (assuming enough data were collected), we might say that the correlation between the police and the traffic jams is no coincident. However, it is another thing to claim that the police "cause" traffic jams; this is something we need to be careful of. The correlation between the two might not be causal. Rather, the correlation might be caused by a third variable.

Now, it is getting more confusing. The traffic jam might be caused by an accident; the police might be directing the traffic because of the accident. The worse the accident, the more police will be out directing traffic to resolve the situation; and the worse the accident, the worse the traffic jam. But without the third variable, we could have concluded that the police cause traffic jams. In fact, if the police hadn't done their jobs, the traffic might have been even worse. In addition, the traffic might be a result of other causes such as rain and flood – and that is why more police might have to come out and work. As a matter of fact, it might be "the traffic jam that causes the police to come out and work,"

Therefore, you cannot jump to the conclusion that one performance measure has an effect on another simply because there is a correlation between the two. We have to do something extra in order to prove the logic behind the correlation. The easiest thing you can notice is that the cause must always come before the effect. Brand awareness performance measure has to increase before sales performance measure – that "could be considered" as logical. However, the other way around would be the end of all. If sales were to increase before brand awareness, we would not be able to conclude that brand awareness increases sales, as the effect cannot precede the cause.

However, an increase in brand awareness that is followed by an increase in sales still does not guarantee the causation. That is why I used the phrase "could be considered." In order to validate, we have to "make an experiment." An experiment would allow us to hold other variables constant, while changing only one variable that we are interested in, to see if the change is significant or not.

If we want to see whether advertisements could increase brand awareness or not, we have to keep other variables constant - do not give a discount or hire more salespersons, for instance.

Then, see if the increased brand awareness could help generate more sales or not. If you are really going to conduct an experiment, you have to design it well, because controlling other variables is not an easy task. However, it is not impossible. Now, I do not want to turn this book into a research-based book. So, I just want to conclude by saying that before jumping to conclusions after seeing a correlation, you have to consider other possible variables that might be the cause first.

Can you hear what KPI is telling you?

Reading this title, many of you might be concerned that something might be wrong with me. Am I too obsessed with performance measurement that I am actually talking to it? Not at all. You can relax now. I am just fine. What I mean is that if we do not carefully analyze the result of a performance measure, we might miss a lot of things. Let's take a look. Assume that the percentage of defect performance measure is as follows:

Round 1: 10%
Round 2: 5%
Round 3: 3%
Round 4: 2.9%
Round 5: 2.85%

If we simply look through it, we might think that our performance is improving. Moreover, if we only take a look at the values round by round, we would only be able to conclude that the percentage of defects is gradually decreasing. However, if we carefully analyze these numbers, we would see that these performance measure values are trying to tell us something. We can see that in the first rounds, the amount of decrease is greater.

Later on (round 3 onwards), the numbers are still decreasing but at a much slower rate, even though same amount of resources or effort is spent.

Why is that? The process that we are trying to improve is reaching its improvement limit. The process will not improve any further if we keep using the same method. We need to change the process or come up with new ideas to see dramatic improvements. This is where many people make mistakes. They invest their resources and effort on things that are reaching their limit of improvement. More importantly, the result of the performance measure might have already told us that, but we just might not have listened. So, go back and take a look at your performance measure values to see if they are indicating anything like this.

Do not analyze results separately.

Sometimes when you analyze each performance measure separately, you do not get anything out of it. Let me give you an example. Let's say we have two performance measures: the number of tasks employees can finish per week and the task error rate (in percentage). Analyzing them separately might lead to the following conclusions.

The number of tasks employees can finish per week has gradually increased since the first week of the year until the 10th week. We might conclude that our employees have worked very hard, which is why the number of tasks done has continuously increased. The second one, the task error rate, has remained stable until the 6th week when the error rate has started to gradually increase. We might conclude that after the 6th week, the error rate started to increase because our employees began to work negligently. Also, it does not seem like the rate will decrease anytime soon.

After this analysis, each department would fix their own problem independently. However, if we analyze performance measure number 1 and 2 together, we might be able to get something useful out of them. During the first weeks (weeks 1-5), our employees were able to work more. However, the error rate was low and stable, which means that the employees still did not work at full capacity. But the important point is about the 6th week when employees still managed to finish more work. However, working more always comes with more errors. Or simply put, employees could finish more work because they reduced the quality of their work. We can imply further that the true capability of our employees lies upto the 5th week, because despite the fact that they were able to finish more work after the 5th week, they did it by compromising quality. This is just an example. Try analyzing two performance measures together, and you might come across something even more interesting than siloed results.

Analyze performance measure to identify capacity.

"Can I hire more people?" Many of you might have heard this kind of complaint before. Most of the time, these complaints have valid reasons. They really do not have enough people, and need assistance. However, most of the time, this is not the case. The person who complains the most might not be the busiest one. Sometimes the one who says nothing is the busiest one, needing help the most. This person is just too busy that he or she has no time to complain. What I am trying to say is that sometimes performance measures could prove something. For example, you can use a performance measure to test if your department is working at its fullest capacity or not.

Testing something like this with machines would be very easy, because machines never slack off or complain. With or without an inspector, they would still work at their highest capacity. Human work capacity, on the other hand, is more complicated, because people could work fast sometimes and work slowly at other times – sometimes they are on fire, sometimes dispirited.

One of the methods to help estimate such outcome is through an appropriate performance measure. Let's assume we want to estimate the capacity of a certain department that mainly uses human labor. We can start off by listing all of the tasks this department is responsible for. Then, we can estimate the amount of time needed to finish each task. For example, if our employees have to contact clients, we would have to estimate how much time they would need to spend on a client. Let's say it is approximately 10 minutes each. After that, we could collect data for a week (5 business days). For example, if we know that the department contacted 600 customers this week, we could calculate the amount of time this department spent working, which is 600 x 10 = 6,000 minutes. Then, we could find the total amount of time. Let's say there are five employees in total. Each of them work 40 hours a week. Hence, the total time would equal 5 x 40 x 60 = 12,000 minutes.

For the last part, we have to find the percentage the employees spent working, which equals 6,000/12,000 = 50%. We can roughly see that this department works only half of the time they have. If this department asks for more people, we would need to ask them why, given such percentage. Therefore, performance measures could be another good source of information when it comes to finding out work capacity.

If you change your perspective in analysis, you might see things differently.

What I am going to write about for this topic is a simple technique that will make you look at performance measurement results differently. First things first, each department has their own performance measures. Why is that so? Most organizations have an organizational structure that is divided into various departments; the performance measures are correspondingly divided.

So, what is wrong with dividing our organization into different departments? I have to say that in fact there are some advantages for doing things this way. We would get to see the performance of the department we work for. However when you look through the eyes of each department without involving other departments, this thing called "sub-optimum" can happen. Sub-optimum is an attempt to make our department's performance measurement result look best, without caring about other departments.

Let me give you an example. If our department gets measured in the amount of time we spend serving a customer, of course, management would want us to work hard to reduce this number. What could happen is that when a customer who has complicated problems comes asking for assistance and although we know exactly how to solve the problems, instead of trying to immediately solve the problems, we would suggest the customer to contact another department as we also know that solving the problems would take a lot of time, which would make our performance measurement results look bad. Our performance measurement result might end up looking good for our department, but this is definitely bad for the company.

Therefore, in addition to analyzing the data from the perspective of each department, we should look at the process. In the case above, we should also analyze the total time spent from when the customer walks in until the problem is solved, so that we will be able to see the results from another perspective. This will definitely help the organization as a whole.

Analyze the result like you are taking a photo.

There is a particularly useful camera function, which I believe many people have already tried before: zooming. Sometimes we zoom in, sometimes zoom out. No one always zooms in to get close-up photos. And likewise, no one always zooms out to capture only tiny humans with the surrounding scenery. Same goes for performance measurement analysis – we have to both zoom in and out. Zooming in means to analyze each performance measure in detail, because sometimes when we only look at the index, we might not get anything out of it. Just like simple mathematics, when we add up the values of many performance measures to create an index, the rate of change of that particular index would gradually decrease. Or simply put, it would remain stable. However, a stable index does not imply that every performance measure is stable; some might increase while others decrease. By zooming in, we would be able to see a much clearer picture.

Management needs to zoom out as well. Zooming out means to look at the overall picture instead of analyzing each performance measurement value. There is a saying, "not seeing the forest for the trees." It explains everything. To zoom out is to look at the past in order to predict the future of the whole organization. So, try to adapt my suggestions to your organization, and do not forget to zoom in and zoom out.

Look at both opportunities and threats.

Let me start off by telling you about two incidents.

Incident 1

Boss: "Why didn't we reach our sales goal? We're still 50% short."

Subordinate: "Because right now, the quality of our product is lower, we've received many customer complaints."

Boss: "If that's so, let's find a solution with the production team."

Incident 2

Boss: "We did great this time. Look, our sales are 50% higher than the goal."

Subordinate: "You should treat us to a meal then."

Boss: "Of course. Tell me when, and we'll go celebrate."

These two incidents might seem ordinary at first sight. However, if you consider the details, you would see that people are only worried when there is a problem, but never realize potentially missed opportunities. In the first incident, the company is 50% below the goal. The company might begin to worry and try to find a solution, which is a good thing that could lead to improvements. Whereas in the second incident, the company overachieved the goal by 50%, so they celebrated their success without knowing why the sales have exceeded the goal so much.

Surpassing the goal by 50% is something to be proud of for sure, but we should pay careful attention to the rationale behind it in terms of strategic planning. In this case, the company's overachievement might simultaneously indicate that the company might have set the bar too low. Therefore, the resources that were delegated to achieve the goal was also too low, despite vast opportunities in the market. If the company were able to set a more accurate goal, they would have delegated more resources that would have improved the outcome. Instead of finding the reasons behind bad performance measurement results, asking *why the outcome is highly different from the goal* might give you some useful insights.

Analyzing a pair is better than analyzing an individual.

Sometimes analyzing two performance measures together could give you interesting data. Here's an example. Let's say the value of the quality index has increased, while the value of productivity index has decreased (productivity = output/input). In this case, if we analyze the two performance measures separately, we would not get much useful information out of our analysis. We might try to find supporting evidence for what we saw. For example, why has quality improved? Because of this and that... Why has productivity fallen? Because of this problem and that problem - or something along these lines.

However, if we analyze both performance measures together, we might find out that the reason why quality has improved while productivity has fallen is not because we have fixed the problem at its root cause, but rather because we have been working on the same tasks repeatedly. We might try to use better quality control. And once we are able to identify the problem, we would work on the problem over and over again, until the quality problem is eliminated, making quality performance measures look better (product return rate would be reduced, for instance). However, we have added so much input (such as labor) that it causes productivity (output/input) to decline.

What should we do if we find that quality performance measure has improved and the quality problem has been dealt with, but still productivity has not increased at all? Many people have faced this problem before, and many might wonder why such a thing has happened? If the quality is better and the problem is eliminated, why doesn't productivity improve? The reason is that once the problem has been solved, we would have leftover resources. We might not have utilized those resources to the organization's advantage. Let me give you an example. In the past, there was a problem with our process, which was why we had to redo everything all the time. It used to take us 8 hours to manufacture one product, but we solved the problem, and it only takes us 6 hours now. Is that better? Yes, it is. But now the question is what did we do with the extra 2 hours? If we don't do anything, productivity will not improve.

See how analyzing two performance measures together can make things much more interesting? Now let's assume that we find out that both quality and productivity have improved. What does it mean? It means we are on the right track. However, it does not mean we could not improve further. We have to continue to identify if there is anything we have not fully utilized in production (after solving the quality problem.)

However, discovering that both quality and productivity performance measures are low, is clearly a bad thing because it shows that we really have problems. But if we have decent performance measures, we should be able to identify the source of the problem, and solve it before it could get any worse. In summary, analyzing two (or more) performance measures at the same time will help you get a clearer picture – it is obviously better than analyzing each performance measure individually – "two is better than one."

Analyze the coherence between strategy, operation, and profit.

Performance measurement results usually reflect the connection between each performance measure. Generally speaking, if our organization has a strong strategy and good operations, we should be able to generate more profit. Conversely, if our strategy and operations were poor, our profit would be low – we might even incur loss.

Let me give you an example. If we have invented a very interesting product (good strategy) and the cost per unit is very low (excellent operation), our profit would increase. However, if we manufacture a product that customers do not like (poor strategy) and the cost per unit is low (excellent operation), we should be able to generate some profit, but it might not be much. If we manage to produce a very interesting product (good strategy), but the cost per unit is very high (poor operation), the profit will not be that higher either. Lastly, we manufacture a product that customers do not like (poor strategy) and the cost per unit is high (poor operation), you should be able to guess what would happen to the profit. We might even incur loss. What I am trying to say is that even though strategy and operations might lead to certain financial results, it might take some time. You should keep this in mind when reading performance measurement results.

Analyze to prioritize.

When we collect data from our performance measures, apart from the results, we would also receive another important data, which is the "priority" of those performance measures. Many of you might have some experience in measuring customer satisfaction. And what you are likely to find out is that the customers are satisfied with many aspects, and there are still many other things that customers are dissatisfied with. And this is where a problem usually arises – sometimes there are many dissatisfied customers, while we have limited amount of resources. So, which problem should be resolved first? Some people might say, "Choose the one with the lowest score." But here's what is interesting: *The thing that customers are most dissatisfied with might not be the thing that the customers give the highest priority to.*

If we measure the level of importance of each topic, we would be able to analyze and make decision easier. There are four possible scenarios:

1) High satisfaction; customers give high priority.

    This means we have done an excellent job. Our strategy would be to maintain this level of satisfaction.

2) High satisfaction; customers give low priority.

    Many might perceive this as totally fine because we have done well anyway. However, this is where you are wrong. We might have spent too many resources in the aspect that customers do not give priority to. What we should do is to reallocate our resources to improve things with higher priority.

3) Low satisfaction; customers give low priority.

    Many people might panic when they see low customer satisfaction scores. However, if the customers do not give importance to that particular aspect, you could relax a little. It means that we could solve this problem when we have surplus resources, because customers do not give high importance to this aspect. This is where we can prioritize which problem should be solved first and which problem should be solved later.

4) Low satisfaction; customers give high priority.

   We need to work on it immediately by using our resources to solve it or reallocating our resources from the less important aspect to fix this problem first.

This is another example, which proves that result analysis can really be beneficial.

Compare to your plan.

We frequently forget comparing our performance results to the plan we had made. Some might ask why it is necessary to do such a thing because we would not be able to fix it anyway. What's done is done, the results are here, why should we compare them with anything at all?

There are two main benefits of comparing results with the predefined plan:

1) It would make us seek for the reasons why we could not follow the plan or why we had overachieved. Identifying the source of problems or opportunities help us solve problems or recognize opportunities better in the future.

2) We could plan ahead even better. It is true that no plan could be 100% accurate; but even if the plan fails, we can learn from our mistakes, which would help us improve.

Do not forget to review performance measurement results and compare them to your plan.

Many heads are better than one.

With this headline, I am talking about another technique that I would like to introduce for when you want to analyze and interpret performance measurement results. If an analysis is made by one person, usually, the weakness is that the interpretation is from a single perspective. If an accountant writes the analysis, we would only get the accountant's perspective; if an engineer does the analysis, we would only get the engineer's perspective. And do not argue on whose perspective is better, because the quarrel would never end.

My suggestion is to analyze the results as a team. Each person can express their opinions, and we could be quite certain that the analysis is accurate when there is consensus. However, if each team member sees things differently, it could still be useful because these perspectives could serve as a list of explanations, giving you fresh perspectives. An analysis from a team with members from different departments sharing their perspectives could make you see the overall picture better than an analysis performed by a single department could. In addition, the former kind of analysis is more interesting and useful. I would like to ask for only one thing – do not try to compete with each other, because in the end, everyone might end up losing.

Chapter 14
Make your performance measurement system sustainable

Have you ever seen anyone who uses a hammer to saw wood? And have you ever seen anyone who uses a saw to hammer a nail?

What would happen if so? Same goes for performance measurement. If you have it but never utilize it, or use it the wrong way, apart from not creating anything good, it can cause damage. If you want performance measurement to promote sustainable benefits for your organization, what do you have to do? You can get started by reading this chapter.

#1 Consistency is the key.

Performance measurement is like having a girlfriend. If you want her to stay with you for a long time, you have to take good care of her – not only during the early stages of the relationship (the so-called promotion period), only to abandon her after a while. Many organizations do just that. During the early days, they would collect data, analyze the results, and utilize the information to improve their work processes. But after a while, they begin to get bored of it. They measure consistently at first, then it starts to become an on-and-off thing. And later on, they stop measuring altogether.

If such is your plan, then please do not take on performance management at all, because you have to invest labor, time, and money in building a performance measurement system. Using it for only 3-4 months is quite a shame. If you think performance measurement is good and important, then you have to consistently give it attention. The world is very fast-paced nowadays – analyzing performance measurement results once a year is not adequate. Especially, operations should be measured weekly. However, if the measures are meant for the company executives, then once a month or once a quarter should be enough. Do not forget that "consistency" is the key. Do not let your hard-earned performance measurement be forgotten. It would be such a shame.

#2 Good communication is a must.

If you want your organizational performance measurement system to be sustainable, its reports have to be able to grab attention. Here are some interesting techniques that you could use:

1) Only report the data that is *relevant* to the readers.

Do not send less or more than what the readers need. Too few information is, of course, not useful. But the more common mistake is reporting too much information, because people simply report everything that they have. Allow me to compare this to driving a car. Can you imagine what would happen if you had to monitor 200 gauges? You would never look at any of them, because there are just too many.

2) *Arrange* the contents logically.

This part is also important. Creating a good storytelling for what you want to present – explanations for each section, followed by charts and analyses, for instance – would make the report easy to read.

3) Ensure that the readers could *comprehend* the data.

Try to avoid unnecessary jargon If they have to be included, provide their definitions, because if the readers could not understand them, the whole report would have no value at all.

4) Make it as brief as possible.

Most management do not have much spare time. Therefore, good reports should be brief and to the point, but not too brief that the report is incomplete. You just have to ensure that the report is not dragging on. You can start off by reading the report, and see which parts you can remove without losing useful information. If you choose to keep too much information, management might not read your report at all.

Do you have any organizational performance measurement reports to show me? Which kind of report is good? And which kind of report is bad? There are many bad examples out there. Where can we find good examples? I always say that good reports contain two keywords: "simple" and "relevant." If your report has these two qualities, I guarantee that everyone would want to read it. But where's an example of a good report? I would say it is one that you read every day – it is Facebook. For me, Facebook is the world's best report system. And where exactly is my proof? Well, there are billions of people around the world who read contents on Facebook. If you do not call that the best, I do not know what else to call the best.

Let's take a look at "simple" first. Facebook itself is very simple. You do not have to learn how to use it – you can simply sign up, which is very easy, and you can start posting or reading other people's posts. There is nothing complicated about it, right? Moreover, your friends' posts are also very easy to understand. For example, if the caption says, "Holiday, day off," with a beach photo, you do not need any further explanation to elaborate on what it means. I think it is very easy to comprehend.

The next factor is "relevancy." Facebook beats other websites because of this particular aspect. Imagine all of us entering the same website; we would get the same content. No matter how hard that website is trying to categorize its contents or trying to cover every topic, it would not be able to tailor a specific message to each individual. However, for Facebook, each person's wall contains different contents. My wall is different from yours. And you will only receive relevant and interesting information, because that information belongs to your friends. My wall contains information about my friends, and your wall contains information about your friends. Despite the fact that we are using the same website, we would still receive different information. Isn't that awesome? If a report is good, then there is a higher chance for the performance measurement system to be utilized.

#3 Prioritize, prioritize, prioritize.

Setting priorities is vital for organizational performance measurement. The hardest part of management's job is to utilize the limited amount of resources to solve an unlimited amount of problems. Therefore, performance measurement could act as a tool to help management set priorities as to which problems deserve to be solved first and which problems should be solved later, given a limited amount of resources. Using performance measurement, we would know what is important and what is not. It would allow us to allocate the limited amount of resources to fix the most critical problems.

We could divide priorities into short-term and long-term ones. For example, if we are not able not deliver goods to customers in time - no one would argue that this is not important – in the short-run, we have to find those particular goods from somewhere else and deliver them to customers. But in the long-run, this would not be good for the business. We should consider increasing our production capacity in order to support the rising demand. If the analysis from your organizational performance measurement report can reflect the order of priorities, I believe the readers would find it useful. And eventually, the performance measurement would be beneficial to the organization sustainably.

#4 Feedback is important.

Do you want to know your exam scores? I believe that everyone would say, "Yes." However, some students of mine said that they do not want to know their scores for my class. I would laugh and reply, "Deep down, you want to know the score. You just don't want your friends to know how much you scored, am I right?" Performance measurement is like taking an exam. People who get measured would want to know the results. If you do not want them to know the results, then why measure at all? Without the results, people who get measured would never know how they can improve – they would continue to do what they are doing, which does no good for the company.

Thus, valuable feedback should be specific, meaning that you should tell each department how well they perform – in which aspects they do well and which aspects could be improved. Simply stating that, overall, all departments have done a good or bad job would not be useful because departments would not know which areas they need to improve. If they have done a good job, they should receive recognition. You should not complain when they perform poorly, while saying nothing when they do well. More importantly, when they do not perform well, you should not only punish them and find a person to blame. You should be removing the organization's problems, not the employees.

Feedback should be constructive, meaning that people must receive rewards and recognition to continue to perform well. However, this does not necessarily mean that you should compliment your employees when they perform poorly. Rather, what you should do is to tell them why they performed poorly and how they can improve. Do not make complaints that would only hurt employees' feelings, and do nothing to help them improve. We often see this happen.

"You did really bad. Look at the result. I haven't seen anyone who performed this bad before."

"You have been working here for so long, is this the best you can do?"

This is the kind of feedback that does no good. Feedback is vital. If you could provide good feedback, I believe that the chances are high that your organizational performance measurement system will be sustainable.

#5 Rewards and success

A performance measurement system would succeed and be beneficial to the organization sustainably once we add another positive force. When employees achieve something that makes the organization reach or surpass its goal, they would expect to receive rewards. Many people might think rewards only refer to monetary rewards. Various organizations, especially in the public sector, would say that this is the difficult part because of budget constraints. In fact, money is a kind of reward, however, it is not the only kind of reward. Another type of reward that is no less effective than money is recognition.

Most of the time, employees want recognition more than money. Or in some cases, money can demotivate them. Let's take a look at the following example. Assume that I just finished teaching and am about to drive home. It is raining heavily, and I see a group of my students waiting for a taxi, so I decide to stop my car and ask them where they are headed. Once I learn that they are headed the same way as I am, I tell them to hop in for a ride. When I drop them off, they hand me 10 dollars, saying that it is for the ride. Next time, I would not stop to pick them up. You can see from this example that I would prefer a "thank you" more than money. By giving me money, the students would be discouraging me from giving them a ride again. Rewards are another thing that would make organizational performance measurement sustainable.

Cautions of organizational performance measurement

We frequently hear many suggestions regarding how to fully utilize organizational performance measurement. In this postscript, I would like to introduce the cautions – if you do not want your organizational performance measurement to fail, what shouldn't you do?

1) Do not use performance measurement to control everything.

It is true that one of the pros of performance measurement is to create some kind of control system to make employees follow the organization's goals. But do not forget that employees are human, not machines. Everyone wants a certain level of freedom. Not being able to achieve it because of performance measures would make their jobs boring. Working under various performance measures could unnecessarily cause employees stress. In the end, employees would not want to work at all.

2) Do not tie performance measurement to punishment.

We want to eliminate problems from your organization, not employees. This mindset is very important, because we want performance measurement to be a tool to help employees eliminate problems, rather than being a tool to harm them. Tying performance measurement to punishment would do more harm than good. Although punishment is another kind of driving force, it is rather considered as a negative force. Generally, positive force is more popular. For example, when the result of performance measures show a sign of improvement and the organization can generate more profit, employees should receive rewards.

These two cautions are very significant. Be careful not to let these happen to your organization.

Postscript

I hope this book helps you to understand how vital performance measurement is. More importantly, I hope you learn how to design and put performance measurement system to good use. The idea of performance measurement is becoming more and more important. This book might be one of the starting points that helps ensure performance measurement succeeds in organizations. By "succeed," I mean the thing that we planned to measure improves. For example, if we have a customer satisfaction performance measure, then customer satisfaction has to improve. If we have a defect performance measure, the number of defects should decrease.

Enjoy performance measurement!

Bibliography

Sajjanit, C. and Rompho, N. (2019) Measuring customer-oriented product returns service performance, International Journal of Logistics Management, 30(3), pp. 772-796.

Truktrong, S. and Rompho, N. (2019). Comparing the key success factors affecting change operations between state-owned enterprises and private organisations. The 26th European Operations Manangement Association, 17-19 June 2019, Helsinki, Finland.

Truktrong, S. and Rompho, N. (2019) Willingness to Change in State-owned Enterprises and Private Organizations, Change Management, 18(2), pp. 23-36.

Rompho, N. (2018) Operational performance measures for startups, Measuring Business Excellence, 22(1), pp.31-41.

Morita, M., Iwai, C., Rompho, N., and Phadoongsitthi, M. (2017) Comparison of Group Decision Making in Japan, Thailand, Vietnam, and Russia Using a Business Game, Simulation & Gaming, 48(6), pp. 791-813.

Rompho, N. (2017) HC and financial performance with two HRM strategies, International Journal of Productivity and Performance Management, 66(4), pp. 459-478.

Phadoongsitthi, M., Rompho, N., Iwai, C., and Morita, M. (2017) Effects of national culture on group decision making: a comparative study between Thailand and other Asian countries, International Journal of Economics and Business Research, 13(2), pp. 110-133.

Amornpashara, N. Rompho, N., and Phadoongsitthi, M. (2015) A study of the relationship between using Instagram and purchase intention, Journal of Global Business Advancement, 8(3), pp. 354-370.

Boon-itt S. and Rompho, N. (2012) Measuring Service Quality Dimensions: An Empirical Analysis of Thai Hotel Industry, International Journal of Business Administration, 3(5), pp. 52-63.

Rompho, N. (2012) An experiment in the usefulness of a strategy map, Measuring Business Excellence, 16(2), pp. 55-69.

Rompho, N. and Boon-itt, S. (2012) Measuring the success of a performance measurement system in Thai firms, International Journal of Productivity and Performance Management, 61(5), pp. 548-562.

Rompho, N. (2004) Building the Balanced Scorecard for the University Case Study: The University in Thailand. In A. Neely, M. Kennerley, and A. Walters (Eds.). Performance Measurement and Management: Public and Private, 28-30 July

2004, Edinburgh. Stirling: Centre for Business Performance, Cranfield School of Management.

About the author

Professor Dr. Nopadol Rompho

Professor Dr. Nopadol Rompho graduated with a Bachelor of Engineering, majoring in Chemical Engineering (second class honors), from Chulalongkorn University, Thailand; a Master of Science in Chemical Engineering from Oregon State University, USA; an MBA from Thammasat University, Thailand; and a Doctorate of Philosophy (Management) from University of Glasgow, United Kingdom.

Professor Nopadol has work experience in both government and private sectors. He worked as a consultant for many large organizations, and has continuously produced outstanding academic works and research about organizational performance measurement, operations management, and quantitative analysis. He is a founder of ZeeZcore that offers the OKRs software as a service.

Currently, he is a full-time operations management professor at the Thammasat Business School in Thailand, a member of an international editorial board, and a member of many other boards in academic societies in Thailand.

He can be contacted via email nopadol@tbs.tu.ac.th or LinkedIn: Nopadol Rompho

www.ingramcontent.com/pod-product-compliance
Lightning Source LLC
Chambersburg PA
CBHW030632220526

45463CB00004B/1498